"G.B. Shaw once opined, 'Those who can, do; those who can't, teach.' Gordon Tredgold, in his new book FAST, corrects this harsh judgment. Having led numerous highly successful turnarounds in industry and business, he now shares his profound insights to teach the rest of us, and we are fortunate to have such a learned guide! Whatever else you do today, place your order for this delightful success map—and do it FAST!"

- R. David Lancaster, Professor, Bethel University, McKenzie, TN

"Whether you are a business leader, education leader, or church leader, the success principles in Gordon Tredgold's new book FAST will change YOU first and your organization second. FAST picks up where most leadership books leave off, with a brilliant yet simplistic approach to what leaders need most: Focus, Accountability, Simplicity, and Transparency. It's a must read for any leader!"
- Dr. Lynn Wicker, President, Center for Innovative Educational Solutions, LLC and Author of Raising Kids That Succeed!

"I've been an entrepreneur for over 20 years as a business coach and top earner in two MLMs. I've also created many training programs in my time. Never in my career have I come across a system so simple and easy to follow as FAST! For the first time in my career I have a methodology that is easy to implement and duplicate with my teams! FAST takes us back to basics and is a must read for anyone expecting to lead in the business world. Gordon Tredgold's work is pure genius!"

- Kellie Kuecha, Creator of Brand Omnipresence and Monetize Method

"Time has always been a highly valuable asset to leaders. However, the exponential increase in value of that asset is far beyond anything we could have imagined. Top performing leaders must have access to the right skills and tools necessary to perform at the highest level in today's rapidly shifting business world. What Gordon Tredgold has so brilliantly crafted in his book FAST *is exactly what today's leaders need boiled down into a simple, powerful, and highly usable acronym of* FAST.*"*

- Dov Baron, Founder of Full Monty Leadership, Bestselling Author, and Inc. Magazine Top 100 great Leadership Speakers to Hire

"Leadership is the art of connecting varied individuals to achieve a single goal. However, most companies don't realize this; they don't hire effective leaders, and they don't understand "Focus," the first element of FAST. *Reading this book will give any business leader the edge over their competitors, IF they implement it! Fortunately for all us, Gordon has set out the principles of* FAST *so simply that anyone can follow them to achieve seemingly insurmountable, complex goals!"*

- Claire Boyles, Start Up Marketing Consultant, who helps entrepreneurs develop happy, healthy and wealthy businesses, doing the things they love.

"It is essential for today's business leaders and entrepreneurs to be able to rapidly execute. Gordon Tredgold's FAST *lays out a simple, yet powerful, framework for getting to the results you want through Focus, Accountability, Simplicity and Transparency. The* FAST *methodology will allow you to spend less time in the planning stage so that you can move into action mode much sooner."*

- Sharon Hayes, CEO, Frontspace

"'More is less' gets a whole new meaning with Gordon's new book on the FAST approach. This is such a great tool that can make a real difference to organizations—private, public and third sector alike—the individuals within in them, and their stakeholders. However, simple doesn't mean easy (Who wants easy anyway?). This is not a book written simply to be read. It's written to be delivered! It's all about providing a tool that requires true leadership through Focus (What?), Accountability (Who?), Simplicity (How), and Transparency (How far?). So, don't just name-drop it: live it, breathe it, deliver it!"

- Professor Rune Todnem By, Staffordshire University
Editor-in-Chief, Journal of Change Management
Co-author, Managing Change in Organizations (2014)

FAST

GORDON TREDGOLD

FAST

4

Principles Every
Business Needs to
Achieve Success and
Drive Results

NEXT CENTURY
PUBLISHING

FAST

ISBN: 978-1-68102-057-0
Library of Congress Control Number: 2015909292

Printed in the United States of America

This book is dedicated to my wife, Carine.

TABLE OF CONTENTS

FAST

WHAT IF THERE WAS A RECIPE FOR SUCCESS?

By Gordon Tredgold

If there is a recipe for success, it's not well know as the statistics for failure are startling!

60% 70% 80% 95%

◄ Some facts and statistics on why projects fail ►

17% of large IT projects (over $15m budget) go so badly wrong that they threaten the existence of the company

60% of projects fail, they fail to meet their cost, time and quality commitments.

35% of companies abandoned projects, of projects not abandoned 37% failed to deliver the planned benefits.

49% of US federally funded IT projects are either poorly planned, poorly performing or both.

70% of UK Government IT projects failed 2000-2008, wasting $4b

70% of one survey respondents said they knew the project would fail before they had even started

**Based on multiple reviews of IT Projects by various groups such as McKinsey, Oxford University, KPMG, Guardian Newspaper and the US Government Accountability, amongst others, and reviewing over 7000 projects and speaking with over 3000 respondents these were some of the findings.

It's not just IT projects that fail, according to Bloomberg research.

95% of new products introduced each year fail
- Cincinnati research

75% of consumer packaged goods and retail products fail to earn even $7.5 million during their first year.
-Harvard Bus Review

8 out of 10 entrepreneurs starting a new business fail within the first 18 months.

With over 20 years' experience of successfully turning around failing projects, under performing departments and delivering large complex multimillion dollar change programs, I have discovered that 95% of projects are failing for the same 4 reasons. Most of which are completely avoidable.

Common reasons for failure are a lack of

FOCUS

ACCOUNTABILITY

SIMPLICITY

TRANSPARENCY

If we improve our performance in each of these areas, we will significantly improve our results

Recipe for Success

Focus + Accountability + Simplicity + Transparency = SUCCESS

SUCCESS

FOCUS (The "WHAT")
Focus is about clearly defining the WHAT, the Objective.
Many Companies are Focused on the Wrong WHAT.
Cleary define and communicate what success looks like.
Wrong Focus = Failure!

ACCOUNTABILITY (The "WHO")
Accountability is about the WHO.
Who is accountable for doing the work?
Do they know they are accountable?
Do they know what's expected of them?
How will we ensure that they are held accountable?
Get the Right Person doing the Right Job!

SIMPLICITY (The "HOW")
Simplicity is about the How.
Is our Approach clear and easy to understand.
Do we understand the problem?
Have we clearly communicated the solution?
Simplicity builds belief, belief leads to success!

TRANSPARENCY (The "HOW FAR")
Transparency is about knowing How Far we have to go.
Create true and accurate measure of performance.
Transparency aids fact-based decision making.
Without Transparency we need miracles to succeed.
Transparency in to progress motivates our teams!

How you will increase success by using FAST?

By applying FAST you can revolutionize results and put yourself in the top 5% of leaders who are successful, repeatedly.

If you want to know more about FAST email me at

gordon@leadership-principles.com

This book could not have been completed without the help of the following people:

Phil Lee

Carine Cornelis

Dave Thornton

Tarak Patel

Angela Panayotopulos

Tammy Kling

Kellie Kuecha

Sabrina Fajardo

Michelle Colon-Johnson

Claire Boyles

Jane Garee

Paris Walker

And finally, Nigel Risner

It was Nigel who said to me, "So your keys to success are Simplicity, Transparency, and Focus. What about Accountability? Could you include that?"

I said, "Of course. Accountability is of paramount importance, so much so it goes without saying."

To which he replied, "Yes, but if you say it, then you have Focus, Accountability, Simplicity, and Transparency, which gives you FAST."

Hence FAST Leadership was named. It had been there all along, staring out at me.

FOREWORD BY JOHN SPENCE

Much like Gordon, I've spent the last two decades of my life traveling upward of 200 days a year worldwide to help businesses and executives be more successful. From the top of the Fortune 100, to mom-and-pop shops, to brand-new startups, I've worked with hundreds of companies that have taught me some incredibly important business success (and failure) rules. I also read more than 100 business books a year, constantly looking for new ideas, tools, and techniques that will work in the real world. The book you hold in your hands right now is one of the few I have read that cuts through the clutter and complexity and helps you run a highly successful business.

Several years ago, a Fortune 100 client asked me to put together a keynote address on "The Essence of Excellence." He told me I would have twenty minutes in front of 1,600 employees and he expected a standing ovation—no pressure. I spent weeks preparing for that brief talk. I called CEOs and successful entrepreneurs I had worked with in the past; I called the presidents of colleges and universities where I had lectured; I looked back over my reading material and notebooks, and boiled it down to what I call the Three Watchwords of Excellence.

FOCUS

DISCIPLINE

ACTION

You must focus intently on your philosophy of success, your strategic plan, your driving vision and purpose. Then you must have the discipline to say no to distractions, and do the things you need to do to pursue your vision. Finally, the results you achieve will be directly proportionate to the amount of action you apply. I developed that idea ten years ago, and when Gordon sent me a draft of this book to read, I realized he had created an elegant process and framework for actually achieving those three steps. It's one thing to understand an idea; it's a completely different thing to be able to apply it consistently with discipline. In the following pages, Gordon masterfully illustrates exactly what is necessary to build and sustain a highly successful business.

It's also important to note that he has adhered to what I feel is one of the most important things we can do as business leaders: *make complex things simple.* I meet so many people who make running their businesses far more complex than needed. They have out-of-control organizational charts, fifty-seven key metrics, fourteen strategic objectives, and a proprietary IT system that's constantly going down. What Gordon will show you is that simplicity rules! Keep it simple, keep it focused, keep it running smooth and highly profitable.

He also addresses the single biggest problem my clients face: lack of accountability and disciplined execution. There is absolutely no shortage of truly bright people, savvy strategists, and highly innovative business thinkers, but thoughts don't pay the bills. To be successful today, you must be able to take ideas and turn them into action by creating a culture of accountability that is relentlessly focused on delivering the required business results. This book will show you how to do just that.

Finally, he covers the second biggest problem that every client I have ever had struggles with: lack of open, honest, robust, and transparent communication (which in large part creates the lack of accountability and effective execution). It is impossible to calculate the amount of time, energy, and money wasted by so many organizations because they do not share the necessary information across their organizations. Knowledge is NOT power, but sharing knowledge allows you to empower other people, which is how you leverage your power. Clear, consistent, and transparent communication is essential to the success of every organization, and Gordon's going to help you with that too.

Get ready to take lots of notes and do some serious thinking about your business. Gordon has compiled twenty years as a global leadership expert into the pages that follow. It's your job to figure out which ones will work for you and your business, and then apply them with passion and vigor.

I wish you every possible success,

John Spence

One of the top 100 Business Thought Leaders in America, top 100 Small Business Influencers in America, and top 500 Leadership Development Experts in the World.

INTRODUCTION

In two decades of leadership consulting for some of the world's top companies, I've learned a few things. One is that there truly is a formula for success. It's this formula that will separate the winners from the losers in the decades to come.

The formula is:

Focus + Accountability + Simplicity +

Transparency = Success

In the old days everyone wanted to know, "How can we go from good to great?" But a new day is here, and it's no longer appropriate to ask that question. Perhaps you've already gone from good to great. Now what?

It isn't prudent to rest and observe from the sidelines, with competitors lurking in the shadows. Or perhaps you're involved in turning around a culture, faced with organizational challenges, or in a company that is not even good yet but striving to be. Wherever you are on the spectrum of leadership, you know one thing for sure: if you want something that you've never had before, you must do something that you've never done before.

In the pages to follow, I'll guide you through the important management methodology of FAST.

FAST—the fast-track strategy to success based on the
principles of Focus, Accountability, Simplicity, and
Transparency—is not a dry, academic theory.

It is an approach that has been tried and tested countless times, and one that I have seen in action over and
over again in organizations around the world. These
principles have become the foundation of my life. In
large part, they are what have helped to completely
transform me from a helpless underachiever to a passionate overachiever. FAST changes individuals. FAST
transforms and connects teams.

What is the one thing you want to achieve in this com-
ing year?

Deploy FAST, and I boldly guarantee you will achieve
it. The principles in FAST propelled me forward to
achieve anything and everything that I set my mind to,
from business ventures, to heartwarming sustainable
relationships, to marathon medals.

Since I've immersed myself in these principles, I've introduced the techniques to my family, friends, clients, and
business partners and allies, helping them to streamline
their strategies and revolutionize their attitudes in order
to attain their own personal and professional goals. For
decades, I have used these four principles to revamp
underperforming departments and to resurrect failing
projects in many different industry sectors.

Why Do We Fail?

I was always the guy who volunteered, was selected, or was the only person stupid enough to take on the more difficult assignments. You know, the ones everybody else steered away from. These were the jobs that people ran from because they were thought to be too complex, too constricting in their time frames, or just plain impossible. These are the kinds of jobs I love.

Why? Well, these types of projects and tasks—the ones no one else wants—give you a certain degree of freedom. You have more liberty to break the rules, change the approach, and take chances that otherwise wouldn't be possible or acceptable. Furthermore, I know that if you tackle them head-on with a can-do attitude, you're halfway there. For the most part, we self-prophesize and predict our own triumphs and failures through our attitudes and behavior. Believing that a project is doomed from the get-go is pretty close to signing its death warrant.

The statistics for failure are mindboggling. Over 60 percent of projects fail. In fact, over 80 percent of first-time businesses fail within *the first 18 months*.[1]

After over twenty-five years of leading large transformation programs on an international scale in a number of industries—banking, utilities, logistics, and manufacturing, to name a few—I've reached the conclusion that about **95 percent of failures result from one of two reasons:**

---

[1]   http://www.forbes.com/sites/ericwagner/2013/09/12/five-reasons-8-out-of-10-businesses-fail/

1. We're doing the wrong job.

2. We're doing the right job poorly.

In my experience, the number of these failures could drastically be reduced, if not completely eliminated, by focusing on the four elements that failing businesses seem to lack most: Focus, Accountability, Simplicity, and Transparency.

Incredibly enough, none of these businesses stopped long enough to ask a few basic but groundbreaking questions: **what, who, how**, and **how far?**

Just by stopping to ask these four questions, I've improved the clarity, communication, and performance of hundreds of businesses. Today, my approach is used to successfully implement multi-million-dollar projects and run multi-million-dollar department budgets. Leadership is ultimately about delivering results and achieving goals. That's what you get paid for, that's your calling, and that's your passion.

Defining Excellence

*"We are what we repeatedly do. Excellence then is
not an act, but a habit."*
—Aristotle

As you'll learn in the chapters of this book, there is a key difference between *effectiveness* and *efficiency*. One does not automatically equal the other. Performing poorly on the right task constitutes poor effort. Doing a great job on the wrong task results in wasted effort. Doing a poor job on the wrong task is the least useful of all. Yet when you increase both your effectiveness and your efficiency, you achieve *excellence*—the result of doing the right job extremely well, over and over again. Your implementation of all four interconnected principles—Focus, Accountability, Simplicity, and Transparency—automatically increases both your effectiveness and your efficiency, thereby ensuring excellence.

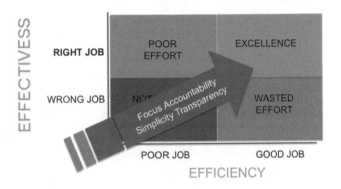

Here they are in a bit more detail:

1. In **FOCUS**, you'll learn to distinguish what the "right job" is, and what success looks like to you. It is the first and most important principle, because it determines your effectiveness. You'll learn the secrets to prioritizing without overextending yourself or your team. You'll discover how to arm yourself and aim with the *very best* chance of hitting the bull's-eye every time. By keeping your eyes on the prize, you'll always know what you're aiming for.

2. In **ACCOUNTABILITY**, you'll discover the high cost of unaccountability and the immediate benefits of responsibility. You'll analyze the best strategies to claim accountability, and the best ways to expand a culture of accountability throughout your entire business. You'll seize

control by learning how to prophesy your own success and make that an inevitable reality. Accountability begins with the individual, and it is absolutely imperative for a healthy business.

3. In **SIMPLICITY**, you'll see how clear communication always ensures better progress and quicker success. You'll debunk why we typically resist simplicity, how we underestimate it, and how you can unleash its transformative power—in ten steps with direct results—to completely revamp your life and your business. You'll instill belief and confidence in your team(s) by learning to communicate simply and clearly, and ensure excellent performance by pointing everyone in the same direction. Simplicity is power.

4. In **TRANSPARENCY**, you'll uncover why you are the heart and the head of your business, and how you can use this to your greatest advantage. I will share the risks and benefits of transparency, and show you how to differentiate the two. It isn't enough to work hard and focus on the right job; you have to understand how to track performance and measure results, further enlightening and motivating the people surrounding you by defining—and approaching—success. Mastering this last principle, you will be able to fully execute the FAST strategy to your best advantage, regardless of your industry.

There is beauty, too, in the reciprocity of these principles. Improvement in one principle automatically correlates to other areas.

For instance, the simpler we make our approach, the easier it will be for our teams to focus. By improving transparency, it's easier to hold people accountable; we'll have clear measurements of their performance and results, and can provide feedback as to whether expectations and time frames are being met. Given the nature of this pattern, even small improvements in each area can snowball to greatly increase overall performance.

Simple, right? Too easy to be true?

Remember that "simple" is not "easy." FAST is not a quick-fix solution, although it *does* reward you with several immediate benefits. It isn't the aspirin you take for the pebble in your shoe. It's the sitting down and extracting of the pebble. It takes more time, more dedication, and more thought. But at the same time, it yields far more fruitful and sustainable results. It enables you to create permanent changes to your operational performance, which will in turn enable you to achieve your goals more quickly and more effectively than ever before.

The FAST Track to Success

The incredible power of this approach, and its consequent usefulness, lies mostly in its accessibility. It is simple and easy to implement, and is applicable to any industry and lifestyle. If you want to be a part of the 20 percent who succeed—who know *why* they are succeeding, and thus have the ability to succeed over and over again—then keep reading. If you want the best for yourself, your company, and your clients, with win-win-win results, then keep reading. However, before effectively implementing FAST, it is important to understand it.

Easier said than done, I know.

The purpose of this book is to share the concepts that have helped me climb professional and social ladders, and have helped others climb alongside me. Please, don't just read this book. Study it. Do the exercises, research the anecdotes, and follow the steps of these strategies. Once you have immersed these four principles into your own business and your own life, share this knowledge and power with your peers, your team(s), and your friends and family.

You wouldn't have picked up this book if you hadn't already realized there is another way—*a better way*—of succeeding. A more effective way, which isn't based on luck and isn't built atop a pyramid of corpses. FAST is this tremendously underrated, tremendously competitive edge. This path is one upon which you make your own luck, you are your own hero, and your pyramid is made of outstretched arms where people scale to the top by pulling others with them.

F = Focus

*"If you don't know where you are going, any road
will get you there."*
–Lewis Carroll

In any aspect of our lives, personal or professional, "focus" can be summarized in one theme, one meaning, and one word: what.

Focus is all about clarifying the questions concerning *what* we're doing. The only way we can align ourselves with our purpose is by being aware of, believing in, and ensuring that this "what" is what we want to be striving toward.

The most important steps of your journey aren't the quickest or heaviest steps; they are the ones that are pointed in the right direction. Whether you are crawling or flying, those steps are the only ones that will get you to your destination.

→ *What* are you doing?

→ *What* is your objective?

→ *What* are you aiming to achieve?

→ *What* does success look like for you?

As leaders, it's critical that we are clear about our "what."

It is exactly this clarity that will allow us to communicate it clearly to our teams, so that we can establish an essential common understanding. It is this clarity that we are obligated to find. In the words of Peter Drucker, "Management is doing things right; leadership is doing the right things."

When we have the wrong focus, it doesn't matter how many hours we put in, how hard we toil, or how efficient we are. We won't taste success, and we'll end up frustrated, demotivated, and burned out, and dragging our teams down with us.

If we are not aiming at the right target, we will inevitably fail.

CHAPTER 1

Misaligned Focus: A Multi-Billion-Euro Blunder

"It is not enough to be busy; so are the ants.
The question is: what are we busy about?"
–Henry David Thoreau

In May 2014, France's national rail operator (SNCF) astounded the world with the world's latest epic engineering failure. It began with the best of intentions, as part of a 15-billion-euro makeover of the French Regional Express Trains (TER).[2] The designs were specified by the state-controlled SNCF. They were quick to deliver 341 of the new 1,860 trains.

The result is perhaps best summarized in a French satirical cartoon by Canard Enchaîné: a crowd of commuters standing along a bustling railway platform, listening to this overhead announcement: "The Paris-Brest train is entering the station. Please pull in your stomachs."

---

[2]   http://www.bbc.com/news/world-europe-27497727

That's right. Due to a tragic and embarrassing over-sight—a very misaligned focus—the 2,000 trains don't fit in the platforms.[3] Although the teams had done an excellent job of delivering the trains safely and on time, they'd delivered against an incorrect specification. They'd done a wrong job very well.

The absurd error was a result of misinformation and miscalculation.

The national rail operator, focusing just on the actual creation of the trains, completely overlooked the obvious: not all railway platforms in France were built at the same time or of equal dimension. The platforms that were built more than fifty years ago were created for slimmer trains, while those built less than thirty years ago are of much wider dimensions. This major issue was discovered too late. In many of the stations, the problem is just a matter of a few *centimeters*…perhaps the most expensive centimeters that France will ever pay for.

It doesn't matter how efficiently you tackle the wrong job, or how quickly you finish the wrong job, or how excellent or beautiful the end result of the wrong job appears. This doesn't change the fact of the matter: it's still the wrong job.

It doesn't matter how powerful or beautiful or smooth-sailing your new trains are; what good are they to you if you can't use them? If you're not focused on the right target, you are doomed to fail in your desired outcome.

Now let us look at the cost.

---

[3]   http://www.the-american-interest.com/2014/05/22/2000-new-french-trains-wont-fit-in-french-stations/

As a result of these miscalculations, some 1,300 platforms need to be adjusted and trimmed, an ordeal that is projected to cost between 50 and 150 million euros (possibly even more).[4] Now while this is a hefty sum, I suspect that the budget would be sufficient to cover the cost increase in the context of their 15-billion-euro project; it represents less than 1 percent of the total costs, and they'll probably have a contingency budget available. There are far more expensive consequences to this story. Look at the impact that this will have on the customers; 1,300 rail stations will need to be at least partially closed in order for the corrections to be made. That won't make many people happy. And the only thing worse than the price tag and the disruption, perhaps, is the ridicule. I certainly wouldn't want to be the project manager accountable for this fiasco.

Looking on the bright side, at least we won't have to "mind the gap."

A Generation of Lost Focus

We live in a high-pressure, information-saturated era. From the moment we wake up to the second that sleep overtakes us, we are bombarded by questions, data, and messages from the world around us. We face demands to make important decisions with little or no time to digest or even think before deciding. Life's soundtrack has become a medley of keyboard clicks, ringtones, and the endless outpouring of thousands of

---

[4]   http://www.hindustantimes.com/world-news/engineers-forget-to-check-space-between-platforms-new-french-trains-too-wide-for-stations/article1-1221659.aspx

television channels and radio stations. Online, there's infinite information at our fingertips—some of it extremely valuable, some of it completely useless, and all of it threatening to overwhelm us. We're exposed to nonstop marketing campaigns, social media updates, and an overload of choices. Even in our dreams, we are processing and mulling over the thoughts and themes of the day.

The Information Age? More like the Misinformation Age.

Don't get me wrong. Variety is essential. But do we really need to choose between 400 shades of blue shampoo bottles? How can we clearly choose our focus—or even remember the necessity of focusing—when we are completely overloaded?

Research shows that your retina communicates to your brain at 10 million bits per second. It's been argued that our brains can take in as much as *400 billion bits* of information per second, but we're only consciously aware of about 2,000 of those bits.[5] In fact, *The MIT Technology Review* published a study revealing that our brains process data no faster than at 60 bits per second.[6] Despite being bombarded with the equivalent of 174 newspapers of data per day, there's only so much we can humanly process.[7]

---

[5] http://www.wisegeek.com/of-all-that-we-see-how-much-can-the-brain-process.htm

[6] http://www.technologyreview.com/view/415041/new-measure-of-human-brain-processing-speed/

[7] http://www.telegraph.co.uk/science/science-news/8316534/Welcome-to-the-information-age-174-newspapers-a-day.html

If you want to make the most of life, professionally and personally, you have to make the most of your time *and* your focus. In a culture where multi-tasking is encouraged—even expected—it may *seem* as if you are doing more by engaging in many things at once, but you are actually inhibiting your effectiveness and efficiency.

Realize that time is limited, and so are our attention spans.

"Once you learn to truly focus, selectively and unstintingly, you gain true power."
–Gordon Tredgold

Keep your eyes on the prize. Your focus may seem unlimited, but the beauty of it (and the irony) is that your best shot at success emerges when you narrow it. In this chapter, you'll discover the strategy you need in order to awaken this innate ability and attain the success you seek. Once you learn to truly focus, selectively and unstintingly, you gain true power. Over time, this focus becomes second nature to you; like any skill, you perfect it with practice. You will discover that any goal you set becomes attainable and you become unstoppable in your journey to reach it, simply because you do not allow for distractions, obstacles, or a Plan B. You're all-in. You're there. You're committed, dedicated, and focused.

You win the prize by keeping your eyes on it.

CHAPTER 2
Strategic Focus: The Bull's-Eye

"Concentrate all your thoughts upon the work at hand. The sun's rays do not burn until brought into focus."
–Alexander Graham Bell

During their training for the Oscar-nominated 2000 film *The Patriot*, Mark Baker taught Mel Gibson (playing Benjamin Martin) and Heath Ledger (Gabriel Martin) how to shoot a muzzle-loading rifle. Mel Gibson echoed Mark's advice during an actual scene in the movie: "Aim small, miss small."[8] It isn't about aiming small in order to avert risk, as some people think. The point is to define and limit your focus to something extremely important so that you are far less likely to miss it. If you aim at a man and miss, you miss the entire man; if you aim at something more specific (like his heart) and miss, you still hit the man (perhaps his shoulder).

---

[8]   http://www.imdb.com/title/tt0187393/trivia

Increased focus translates to increased chances of success.

To hit the dartboard, aim at the bull's-eye—at the *very center* of the bull's-eye. Deliberate and dedicated focus is what keeps you from spearing the wall or a hapless person who is standing nearby. The French rail operator certainly *focused* on one thing—creating new trains—but miscalculated how these trains would turn out and if they would be suitable in the context of the railway stations. By focusing on the wrong outcome, the company regrettably wasted precious time, energy, and money on a completely unsuitable end result. By failing to focus on the correct goal, they inevitably set themselves up for failure.

Narrowing your focus is not enough if you don't know your target.

How focused are you? Chances are you're focused more on one thing than the other. But are you actually focused on the *right things*?

General Electric: Anything But General

"Lack of direction, not lack of time, is the problem.
We all have twenty-four-hour days."
–Zig Ziglar

Strategic focus is the ability to filter through information and pay attention to what really matters. It's the knob on the microscope or telescope that helps you to clearly discern what's at the other end. It's the flashlight beam in a black tunnel that illuminates the path and saves you from breaking your face against the wall. It's the difference between using a shotgun and a sniper rifle.

It will enable you to avoid or mitigate distractions, and helps promote clear thinking and quality workmanship.

And it is *only* attained when you align your focus with your goal.

Let's take a moment to examine this familiar American household name: GE, the General Electric Company. Widely regarded as one of the world's most successful businesses of the twentieth century, it owes this triumph largely to the revolutionary — and incredibly focused — corporate strategy of its CEO, Jack Welch.[9]

Since taking up his post in 1981, Welch has introduced a new era of quality performance management and internal efficiency. During his two decades of managing GE, he revamped every aspect of performance and efficiency, rallying and encouraging his employees to strive toward their greatest potential. He drove them, regardless of their position or job description, to embrace ambitious goals and to constantly seek methods of improvement. Above all, he led by example.[10]

In order to keep the company focused and aligned with its new goals, Welch also set up systems of assessment, implementing his famous "Fix It, Sell It, or Close It" policy: each division had to be the best or second-best product on the market, otherwise it would be withdrawn. In addition, each department rated its staff members individually in three categories: the top 20 percent were rewarded generously, the middle 70

---

[9]   http://www.businessweek.com/1998/23/b3581001.htm
[10]   http://www.businessweek.com/1998/23/b3581001.htm

percent were encouraged to match the top 20 percent, and the bottom 10 percent were fired.[11]

→ **Business Assessment: "Fix It, Sell It, or Close It."**

→ **Staff Assessment: "Top 20 percent, Middle 70 percent, Bottom 10 percent."**

Jack Welch didn't stop there. He followed in the footsteps of other strategic lions, adopting methodologies such as the Six Sigma method developed by Motorola, Inc. Welch fused these methods to create a new initiative that he implemented into his own company with laser-like focus. This strategy, known as GE's Operating System, entailed strategic planning, human resource management, and financial regulation. It consisted of five major initiatives: Work-Out, Boundaryless Organization, Globalization, Six Sigma, and Digitization.[12]

1. **Work-Out**: A forum encouraging open and honest communication. A cross section of employees from each business meet and speak openly about the management practices in their own sects and departments, without fear of critique or retribution. The group's manager is present at the meeting's end to hear the results and recommendations before making a decision as to what further action is required.

[11] https://www.gsb.stanford.edu/insights/jack-welch-create-candor-workplace

[12] http://www.uni-erfurt.de/fileadmin/public-docs/Mikrooekonomie/Vorlesungsmaterialien/Management/Strategy percent20GE.pdf

2. **Boundaryless Organization**: A blurring of company boundaries to promote teambuilding, education, and performance. It promotes information sharing, cross-business learning, and the integration of key suppliers into the corporation's end-to-end processes.

3. **Globalization**: Transactions with international economies to take advantage of global opportunities, boosting GE's business portfolio. During the 1997 Asian financial crisis, for example, GE invested acquired distressed assets in the area. This allowed them to quickly accumulate quality assets at reduced prices, just as they had during the recessions in the U.S. and Europe in the 1980s and the mid-1990s Mexican crisis.

4. **Six Sigma:** "A comprehensive quantitative system for defining, measuring, analyzing, improving, and controlling every aspect of corporate processes," developed by Motorola. One of the most significant claimed benefits of this system is "its focus on achieving measurable financial results from any project to which it is applied."[13] GE's goal was to reduce defects to 3.4 per million.[14]

5. **Digitization:** In 1999, Welch launched a "destroy-your-business.com" program, encouraging managers to visualize how the "dotcom juggernaut" could potentially crush their businesses. It forced them to consider alternatives and to seek further improvements in internal processing, and

---

[13] http://www.uni-erfurt.de/fileadmin/public-docs/Mikrooeko-nomie/Vorlesungsmaterialien/Management/Strategy per-cent20GE.pdf

[14] http://scm.ncsu.edu/scm-articles/article/six-sigma-where-is-it-now

also paved the way for new profitable market opportunities.

The chart below outlines the performance of GE's shares during three years with Jack Welch at the helm.

Welch definitely knew what he wanted and why he wanted it. He clearly visualized what success looked like, and he knew to what heights he wanted to bring the company. As a result, business boomed, customer satisfaction was at an all-time high, and the corporation's shareholders benefitted from a spectacular shareholder value. GE's stock market value increased 5,096 percent (inclusive of dividends) in the twenty years that Welch led.[15]

That's an average increase of 21.3 percent per year.

→ **In what areas did GE focus?**

→ **What tools and techniques has GE used to improve their focus and performance?**

---

[15] http://www.forbes.com/sites/petercohan/2012/10/10/jack-welch-pot-calling-kettle-black/

→ **What have been the benefits of maintaining this focus?**

→ **How could this approach be applied in your own business?**

Where's Your Bull's-Eye?

"If you chase two rabbits, both will escape."
—Anonymous

Failing to align your focus with your goal is not the only danger. Multitasking—trying to manage several things at once—is another common pitfall. It's like trying to chase two rabbits at once. It might seem doable, and you might believe that you'll end up with more than one rabbit, but you'll most likely end up with none. There's really no way that you can simultaneously run after two rabbits that are racing in opposite directions. That's because it's not actually multi-tasking. It's "task-switching."

Instead of processing information from the television *and* a book, you're split between both and you've processed neither. Your valuable attention and time is expended on switching mental gears, getting and re-getting into the "mind-set" of each task. Information that doesn't make it to your short-term memory can't be processed for the long term, and if you can't retain it, you don't recall it. So by seeking to do and learn more at once, you actually accomplish far less. Personally, I've lost count of the number of times that I've tried to work while watching television, only to find that I've written an email or a report that includes dialogue from the movie I'm watching.

Focusing on too many things spreads thin your brain-power. *Forbes Magazine* points out that our short-term memory can store between five to nine things at once, as long as these are things that do not require much brainpower.[16] That's why it's possible to sing while taking a shower or even juggle while riding a unicycle…but it's impossible to watch the news and study a book and actually retain all of the information from both sources.

So why do we do it?

Well, we feel like we're getting more out of it. We confuse being *busy* with being *productive.* In a recent study at Ohio State University, researchers revealed that we feel more emotionally satisfied when we manage to focus on our homework, watch television, *and* keep up conversations with our friends.[17] It seems very fulfilling to believe that we're *that* incredibly talented.[18] Unfortunately, it's an illusion. This study, like countless others, has also proven that people who engage heavily in multiple tasks simultaneously might feel better, but their results are far worse than those of people who focus on singular activities.

→ **Experts estimate that switching between tasks increases your likelihood of making mistakes by 40 percent.[19]**

→ **When everything is a priority, nothing is really a priority.**

---

[16] http://www.forbes.com/fdc/welcome_mjx.shtml

[17] http://researchnews.osu.edu/archive/multitask.htm

[18] http://www.livescience.com/19983-multitaking-work-bad-feel-good.html

[19] http://www.psychologytoday.com/blog/brain-wise/201209/the-true-cost-multi-tasking

→ **Tackle your tasks singularly and in order.**

When everything is a priority, nothing is a priority."
–Garr Reynolds

One of my managers once told me, "Gordon, these are your six #1 priorities," sagely pointing out how poorly I'd been prioritizing my focus. Forget chasing two rabbits headed opposite ways; I was chasing after *six* rabbits running in different directions. When time is of the essence—which it will be—you'll need to choose *one thing* to focus on first. With six #1 priorities, I had a 1/6 chance of getting it right. More importantly, I had a 5/6 chance of getting it wrong. When I focused on the wrong thing, I set myself up to fail. This applies to teams just as much as it does to individuals; overloading our teams with too many priorities will only make matters worse. Learn to prioritize; otherwise, why use the word *priority* in the first place?

Remember back to a time when you were really focused and passionate about something that you were working on. You seemed to slip naturally "into the zone" or you were "with the flow" or "got in sync" with what you were doing. That's exactly what happened. Once you get into the mind-set and groove of what you're doing, stay there as long as you can until you finish the task—that is when you'll be at your most productive. Pay all your bills together *or* answer all your emails *or* give your undivided attention to the meeting that you're attending.

Pick one task at a time and give it 100 percent.

CHAPTER 3

Align Your Company to Win!

*"The indispensable first step to getting the things
you want out of life is this: decide what you want."*
–Ben Stein

Are You Aligned To Win?

Given that your scope of focus is limited, the most important thing is that you're focusing on the right goal! Of course there are risks. As with anything, there are beneficial and detrimental ways of focusing.

I've seen too many businesses suffer from misaligned focus or overloaded focus. People focus on the wrong outcome or strategy—a mistake that they're usually not aware of—and simply can't reach their goals. The company then demands more from their teams—more time, more effort—but it is fruitless. No matter how hard they work, no matter how efficient they become, they just keep tumbling faster down the wrong path.

Efficient is not the same as *effective*, and all roads *do not* lead to Rome. Not only do the leaders fail to achieve their goals, but they also end up with frustrated and demotivated teams.

As a leader, it is your responsibility to keep a clear head and a clean vision.

Sometimes the pressure of time or stress clouds our visualizations, and we can make mistakes because we're *too close* to the problem. We don't see what's important or what's obvious. It's important to find the time and cultivate the wisdom to step back and check that you and your people are all aligned with the correct goal.

A leader is a guide as much as he or she is a manager.

The alignment should be complete, and ingrained in all the company's policies and departments as necessary. I often see companies that say they are focused on Goals A, B, and C, and yet they reward their staff with bonuses based on the achievements of Goals X, Y, and Z. Which goals do you think the teams will be focused on? Those that benefit them, naturally! You need to ensure that the rewards (e.g., the benefits)—a pivotal part of the mind-set—are aligned with the objectives. Remember, what gets measured is what improves. If we measure the wrong things, then we focus on and improve the wrong things.

> → **Are you focusing on the right things?**

> → **Are you focusing on too many things at the same time?**

> → **Are the rewards aligned with the correct goals?**

At one manufacturing company where I worked, I was asked to examine what could be done to improve performance. They thought they were doing a great job, but a red flag was being waved in their faces: a lot of customer dissatisfaction. The first thing I did was ask to see their performance reports, which would help me gauge their key performance indicators (KPIs) and whether they were focused on the right things or not. The performance manager proudly handed me a folder about two inches thick. "These are the Top 47 KPIs that we measure every month. But it's too much to read through, so we created a management cockpit summary view."

I was bewildered. They were focused on *everything*, meaning they could really focus on *nothing*. It was impossible to see what was going on. It was like being in a jumbo 747 cockpit when all you needed was a little car to drive over to the grocery store.

I met with the business leaders to outline two of the most important things: what was important for them and what challenges they were experiencing. Their devotion to their customers and their desire to cater to them was obvious; they'd come up with forty-seven KPIs, after all. Unfortunately, all these KPIs were interesting but irrelevant. We sat down and categorized the problems into three clean-cut groups: 1.) System availability; 2.) Speed of response; and 3.) Ticket resolution times (how quickly problems were solved). We created service reports based on these three criteria for each of the top seventy applications, with agreed performance levels that we would measure.

Now we were only focused on three things per system. It was doable. Even better, it was incredibly effective. It allowed us to step back and view the entire scope of the business and its customer transactions. It furthermore provided us with a valuable document, which we could easily share with everyone involved in order to discuss the company's performance.

We began to measure with a certain system in place. If any one of the criteria didn't meet the agreed levels (i.e., too many outages, slow performance, or problems that weren't fixed in a timely manner), we set the service report to "red." Initially, we found that the majority of services were being colored red. This enabled us to find and focus on the underlying issues. With root causes identified, we were able to significantly improve performance. Consequently, customer satisfaction began to drastically improve.

After the first year, we also aligned bonuses with service performance, ensuring that we maintained the teams' focus on the right things. Based on our original measurements, the company delivered at a mere 64 percent success rate. By 2012, we'd reached a peak performance, delivering 97.7 percent of the service in line with the agreed performance. Customers had never been happier—and neither had the company!

> *"The prime condition of success: concentrate your energy, thought, and capital exclusively on the business in which you are engaged. Having begun on one line, resolve to fight it out on that line, to lead in it, adopt every improvement, have the best machinery, and know the most about it."*
> *–Andrew Carnegie*

Be careful to lead by example, and take care that you do not set your teams up for multi-tasking. If we give our teams too many things to do—especially paired with insufficient time to do them—it will lead them to prioritizing their own tasks. Without a clear picture of what success looks like, the teams often end up focusing on the wrong things, resulting in overloaded *and* misaligned focus.

As a leader, it is essential that you define your goals and your objectives to the team, and ensure that these are clearly communicated and understood. Guide them to focus on the right things and align them together on the road to success. Listen to your teams! There have been many instances where they have been working on the wrong job and *knew* they were doing so, but *management wasn't listening* to them. Ask your teams what they think is an invaluable investment of your time and effort.

→ **Keep the goals and targets to a minimum** (three to five).

→ **Review the goals and targets.** Make sure that they are clear, simply explained, and well understood.

→ **Review the solution, approach, or process** in detail. Ensure whether it will lead to the desired results, if successfully executed.

→ **Ask a third party to review the solution** (either an external party or an uninvolved internal, i.e., an audit) and check if the focus appears aligned.

→ **Ask each team** whether they think they will be successful (and why).

→ **Communicate clearly, simply, and consistently with each team** to ensure that everyone understands and is aligned with the goals.

Research has shown that, for 75 percent of projects that failed, the teams had predicted failure before they'd even begun the project.[20] Given these statistics, it would be a wise investment to ask each team's opinion to reassess if the right path is being followed. Even if your perspectives differ from those of your team, it's important to understand and address their concerns. By instilling the belief of success in people, we help to transform a negative self-fulfilling prophecy into a positive one.

If we do an open and honest assessment of our focus, it puts us in an excellent position to understand where we are and how we can improve that focus. Once we have the right focus—the right "what"—we can be sure that our aim is true and that we've put ourselves in a position to succeed. With the right focus, we have paved the asphalt for our very own fast-track to success.

Limited Focus, Unlimited Power

"There is one quality that one must possess to win, and that is definiteness of purpose, the knowledge of what one wants, and a burning desire to possess it."
–Napoleon Hill

The FAST Method is the fast-track to success.

Strategic focus is the foundation of this track, built upon your knowledge of and devotion to two things: **what you want and why you want it.** Knowing what you want

---

[20]   http://www.geneca.com/75-business-executives-anticipate-software-projects-fail/

and why you want it is the most basic description of your goal. It is also the most essential. Before you tackle any goal, make sure that you define it. It's hard to get somewhere if you don't know where you're going. It's impossible to find the right solution if you haven't yet defined the problem. And it's impossible to effectively communicate to your team what they need to do if you don't understand what needs to be done.

In order to define any goal, ask these three underlying questions:

→ **What are you doing?**

→ **Why are you doing it?**

→ **What does success look like as an outcome?**

Do you know yourself? What do you want and why do you want it? Discovering and creating ourselves is one of the most basic, beautiful, and complex purposes of life. From the ancient Greeks like Plato and Pythagoras, to modern-day poets and philosophers and scientists, these two words of advice echo through the ages: "Know thyself."

If you want to live a better life, if you want to grow a better business, if you want to become a better version of yourself, begin by asking better questions.

Sometimes the simplest questions unlock the most complicated mysteries. I want you to pause for a moment and complete the following exercise. Consider the most important goal you are tackling in your life right now. Answer the following questions. By clarifying where you're going, you'll align your body, your eyes, and your mind-set so that you are aiming at the bull's-eye. Since this book chiefly addresses leadership in the corporate world, you could begin by defining a business goal. Remember, however, this method can and does apply to all spheres of your life, personal and professional. Incorporating the FAST principles was what enabled me to complete my first marathon, a journey chronicled in my first book, *Leadership: It's a Marathon, Not a Sprint.*

1. **Identify your desired end state.**

    a.   What is my objective? _____

    _____
    _____
    _____
    _____
    _____
    _____

    b.   What does success look like as an outcome?

    _____
    _____
    _____
    _____
    _____
    _____

    c.   What should I be doing to get there? _____

    _____
    _____
    _____
    _____
    _____
    _____

d. What am I currently doing? _____

_____

_____

_____

_____

_____

_____

e. What do I need to change? _____

_____

_____

_____

_____

_____

2. **Consider potential outcomes.**

a. What are the benefits of strategically focusing on my goal? _____

_____

_____

_____

_____

_____

_____

b. What are the risks of focus? _____

_____

_____

_____

_____

_____

_____

3. **Strategize on leveraging your strengths and overcoming your weaknesses.**

   a. What are my strengths? _____

   _____

   _____

   _____

   _____

   _____

   _____

   b. What are my weaknesses and challenges?

   _____

   _____

   _____

   _____

   _____

   c. How do I leverage strengths and overcome weaknesses? _____

   _____

   _____

   _____

   _____

   _____

   _____

"Management is doing things right; leadership is doing the right things."
–Peter Drucker

Harnessing your power to focus is incredible, but you must also ensure that you are focusing on what you really *need* to focus on.

My brother's story from his time in the army always comes to mind when I talk about misaligned focus. He'd been signed up to compete in a ski jump. He was paired up with a new coach, who sat down with him at the top of the jump and instructed him in two things. "Focus on just these two things," the man insisted. First, as he was gliding toward the end of the slope, my brother had to remember to bend his legs and then lunge up in order to take off. Secondly, my brother had to focus on positioning his body in the perfect position so that he'd glide and jump longer.

"Drive and glide," the coach kept repeating. "Drive and glide. Don't think of anything else. Drive and glide. Just drive and glide."

When my brother finally pushed off, his mind was completely focused on *drive and glide*. As he got to the end of the jump, he bent his knees. He did the best drive he could. He lifted himself off the ground. Then he pulled his elbows in and adopted an outstanding position to glide. He felt wonderful, exhilarated—the best jump he'd ever done, he was sure.

Feeling very proud of himself, he looked down, only to see his skis fall off.

With all his focus on *drive and glide*, he'd forgotten to attach his ski boots to his skis. Needless to say, a very promising takeoff resulted in a pretty painful conclusion. A misplacement of focus cost my brother that jump and rewarded him with a good deal of bruising. It's imperative that we focus on the right things and to the right extent. Too narrow of a focus, and we risk losing sight of the forest for the trees; too broad of a focus, and we risk getting lost in the forest.

A = Accountability

*"Accountability is accepting that you are the
source of both the cause and the solution to your
problems."*
–Gordon Tredgold

If *focus* concerns the "what" of our goal, *accountability* refers to the "who." Failures regularly occur because it is never clarified who is accountable for actually getting the job done. Whether this is a personal goal or a professional endeavor, you are the leader of both yourself and your business. So the "who" is, first and foremost, *you*.

→ **Who is going to be accountable for doing the work?**

→ **Does that person know he or she is accountable?**

→ **How will we ensure that he or she is held accountable?**

→ **What are our expectations of the person who is accountable?**

We can share this accountability by delegating responsibilities, but we should never shrug off our personal accountability. If we do, it's typically under the harsh beam of failure, meaning that we are looking for someone to blame. Of course, this method is starkly counterintuitive to success and progress. As a leader, your personal accountability extends as professional accountability toward everyone and everything that you manage. It is the leader's duty to ensure the success of the team, and that is hugely done by embracing accountability.

The leader defines the culture of an organization. If you want that culture to be one where people accept their accountabilities, you must lead by example. The leader must be the role model; you need to show what it means to be accountable. By holding yourself accountable, others will be far more inclined to accept responsibility, and a culture of accountability will consequently flourish. When you assign responsibilities, ensure that you've clearly communicated your expectations and desired outcome, as well as the tasks. Further ensure that you've assigned the correct resources, provided the right skills and tools, and delegated the right levels of authority.

Only after you do that can your team truly accept accountability.

If you do not provide these prerequisites for success, you haven't fulfilled your obligation as a leader. You have failed in motivating your teams to accept accountability, and you have failed to put them in a position that is set for success. By providing these prerequisites, however, you empower your teams to take ownership. The results of inevitable and significant improvement speak for themselves.

CHAPTER 4

The Consequences of Unaccountability

"It is easy to dodge our responsibilities, but we cannot dodge the consequences of dodging our responsibilities."
—Sir Josiah Stamp

In 1625, King Gustav of Sweden decided to commission the construction of what was supposed to become the most stupendous warship in all of Europe.[21]

He commissioned renowned shipbuilder Hendrick Hybertzoon to oversee the creation of what would be called *Vasa*, envisioned to be the Swedish Navy's mightiest flagship. Reportedly, there were no written specifications on the length of the ship. Hybertzoon gathered his resources under the assumption that the flagship would be no longer than the typical 108 feet.

---

[21]   http://vu.bits-pilani.ac.in/Ooad/Lesson1/topic2.htm

The king, however, dead set on creating the most glorious vessel known to Europe, instructed his shipbuilder to elongate the ship to 120 feet after the shipbuilder had already finished the keel. Gustav would not listen to Hybertzoon's warnings that structural changes mustn't be done after the keel and planking had been completed. After rumors that the King of Denmark had commissioned the building of his own flagship with *two* gun decks, Gustav immediately demanded the addition of a second gun deck to his own one-deck flagship. This meant an addition of fifty bronze canons, each weighing a ton. Gustav also wanted to cover the ship with ornate, glorious, and heavy sculptures—and he wanted it all completed months ahead of schedule.

Shipbuilders in those days depended on their ability to make educated guesses, building and learning from their mistakes. No one dared to question the king anymore, despite knowing that all these changes would unbalance and weaken the ship. Hybertzoon died from illness, perhaps collapsing beneath the stress of this impossible task. His brother Arent took over, despite his inexperience. Arent Hybertzoon's calculations did not take into account the extra deck of cannons, cooking supplies, and other items that added to the ship's weight. He later tried to compensate by adding more planking, but there was no room left under the deck for the respective ballast.

The king's patience was running out.

What resulted was a magnificent spectacle of a warship: a flagship that was neither the longest nor the most armed, but formidable in that her cannons on the one side could supposedly, combined, shoot a weight of 588 pounds.[22] Yet what really reigned was *Vasa's* instability. The navy "tested" the flagship by having the crewmen run together back and forth from one side of the ship to the other. They made three such runs. The ship rocked each time, threatening to capsize. King Gustav was not informed of these unacceptable results.

On a calm day in August 1628, Captain Sofring Hansson ordered the *Vasa* to set sail. A few minutes later, the wind filled her sails and rocked the ship. The wind continued to force the ship onto her port side. Water flooded into the lower deck, causing the ship to heel faster and faster. The insufficient ballast shifted, further tilting the ship.

Vasa sunk on her maiden voyage. Dozens of men drowned that day before the eyes of thousands watching helplessly from the shore. The flagship had completed less than one nautical mile.

Accountability: A Foundation of Integrity

"Men holding themselves accountable to nobody
ought not to be trusted by anybody."
—Thomas Paine

What caused the *Vasa's* tragic sinking? Certainly it was, in part, a matter of misaligned focus. Under the demands of King Gustav, the builders prioritized deadlines ahead of quality and successful performance, and they didn't really have a clear picture of what success looked like. Moreover, there was a far greater focus on how the ship *looked* as opposed to how it *functioned*. Thus, it was also an issue of increased complexity, since there were too

---

[22] http://en.wikipedia.org/wiki/Vasa_(ship)

many details and far more additions than necessary than the builders could produce.

Most of all, however, it was a problem of accountability.

King Gustav, despite all his commands, did not hold himself accountable for the ship's seaworthiness; he merely transferred the stress and impossibility of the task onto the builders. The captain in charge of testing the ship did not accept accountability, either, and that, in my opinion, is just as bad. The king asked for the impossible, likely without understanding how unreasonable his demands were. Yet the builder *knew better*. The builder—the leader who was charged with delivering the final product—should have drawn the line at this impossible task. By accepting a job he *knew* would result in failure, he shirked in his accountability. He saw the problem of the rocking ship, knew that the ship would in all probability sink, and yet failed to report it. He did nothing to avoid the calamity and the deaths, even though he knew they would be inevitable.

Sometimes things fall apart just because the "who" isn't clarified. No one knows *who* is accountable for the work, yet no one wants to accept accountability. In your company, you might come across crucial tasks that have been neglected just because someone didn't understand—or accept—that it was his or her responsibility. In soccer, we sometimes see someone score a goal unmarked, only because no one clarified whose job it was to mark the goal scorer. Then there are those instances when people are considered accountable but they don't take that obligation seriously.

In the business world, as in any interpersonal environment or relationship, there are few worse things than the lack of accountability. When no one is to blame, everyone is to blame. We all know or have heard of leaders who repeatedly announce exciting aspirations, visions, mission statements, team goals, and then fail to deliver. Their fate becomes that of the *Vasa*. They sink, taking the rest of their crew with them, into a downward spiral of cynicism, broken trust, and eroding dedication.

So let's clear it up. Exactly *who* is accountable? First and foremost, you are.

Accountability is a path toward success, and it applies to everyone. It's the leader's job—*your job*—to ensure that the stepping stones are all in place. Luckily, we can narrow these down to three simple steps—which makes each step all the more imperative. Our progress, and ultimately our successes, are the result of this three-step process:

→ **Accept tasks**

→ **Do them**

→ **Answer for them**

Take a moment to analyze your personal performance as a leader of the business. How are you doing? How do you tackle any goal? Can you outline your process? Even if you haven't stopped to think about it, you likely have a formula by which you do the things you do. The formula for success always includes accountability; that is the foundation of any business's integrity and character. By practicing accountability, you practice integrity. You seek to constantly improve by monitoring yourself and recognizing your faults. You accept your obligations, your responsibilities, and especially the consequences of your mistakes, which is the first step in learning from them.

Of course, it's not *just* your job; if everyone simply defers to the leader, we end up with a *Vasa*. We need to break down and delegate accountability, but we must remember that we need to begin by setting the example. Leaders are held accountable for the strengths and weaknesses of their team. This accountability is partially shared through your delegation of responsibilities. Each and every member of the team should be held responsible for his or her own particular portion of work. As the leader, you are nonetheless accountable for clearly delegating and communicating these responsibilities so that all parties involved are crystal-clear on what they are doing, what must be done, and what success looks like.

→ **Responsible: You are involved, possibly performing a clearly defined task, and your performance could determine a successful outcome.**

→ **Accountable: You have the obligation to ensure there will be a successful outcome. You may delegate responsibilities.**

Accountability begins with you.

CHAPTER 5

Seven Steps to a Self-Fulfilling Prophecy for Success

"Accountability separates the wishers in life from the action-takers that care enough about their future to account for their daily actions."
–John Di Lemme

According to a study conducted in 2011 by the software development firm Geneca, the majority of people interviewed—approximately 600 business and IT executives—believe, even before the projects have been launched, that their projects will fail. Statistics show that 75 percent of project participants lack faith in their work. This lack of confidence is utterly crippling.[23]

---

[23] http://faethcoaching.com/it-project-failure-rates-facts-and-reasons/

→ 75 percent of project participants expect their projects to fail due to "fuzzy business objectives, out-of-sync stakeholders, and excessive rework."[24]

→ 75 percent of respondents admit that their projects are often "doomed right from the start."

→ 80 percent admit to spending at least half their time reworking the project.

→ 78 percent believe that the business isn't synced with project requirements and needs.

→ 45 percent feel that the business objectives aren't clear enough.

→ More than 80 percent think the requirements process doesn't articulate the business needs.

→ Only 23 percent were always in agreement when a project was completed.

Failure usually happens because we don't consider ourselves the creators of our own successes. If you don't feel responsible for something, you feel that you can't determine the outcome. This stand-off approach implies powerlessness and, thus, a sense of defeat.

This leads us to a stunning conclusion: *we create our own failures.*

As scary or as sad as that may sound, the realization of this is actually pure gold. What it helps us realize is that our approach and our results are often self-imposed; this works as a self-fulfilling prophecy. And just as we can doom ourselves to failure by deciding that we are

---

[24] http://www.businesscomputingworld.co.uk/management-by-osmosis/

helpless to change an outcome, we can just as simply seize control—and seize success—by seizing responsibility. Naturally, this begins by accepting responsibility and holding yourself accountable for whatever you do. It also means sharing accountability and instilling this sense of ownership and responsibility in the entire team. Consider these seven simple steps:

1. Clear Communication

Ensure that everyone involved has a crystal-clear understanding of what needs to be known. Set and define:

→ Expectations,

→ Roles and responsibilities,

→ Vision (desired outcome), and

→ Consequences (positive and negative).

2. Direction

Your role does not end with communicating what you need. You must clarify it and promote direction. It is critical that you provide your people with the resources and tools that they need to be successful. Your job is to deliver the necessary training, encouragement, and guidance.

3. A Solution-Focused Mind-set

→ Do not accept, promote, or practice denial, blaming, or scapegoating.

→ Replace excuses with solutions.

→ Mistakes and missteps happen. Work to ensure that these serve you; transform them from obstacles into lessons.

4. Shared Accountability

Create a culture of accountability where people accept responsibilities and are accountable for their personal actions.

→ Direct *and* delegate. Enforce this accountability. While you are first and foremost accountable, it doesn't mean everyone else is off the hook.

→ Holding people accountable for their own deeds does not mean that you are breeding a culture of confrontation and conflict. By taking responsibilities seriously and delegating them respectfully and thoughtfully, you breed a culture of integrity, cooperation, and success.

→ Remind your people that, while they are accountable for a small part, you are accountable for the overall success; you share a common interest in their success and you will do whatever possible to help them.

5. An Understanding of Accountability

Accountability shouldn't be something forced, nor should you dread holding people accountable.

→ Ideally, people choose to be accountable because they realize the immediate and incredible benefits. The beauty of responsibility is that once you accept a problem as yours, you immediately gain the power to fix it.

→ Once you tackle an area that is clearly within your responsibility, you can take ownership and pride in the results that you generate.

6. Milestones and Metrics

Keep your metrics as clear as your standards. You improve what you measure. If you truly want to see changes in performance:

→ Break down accountability to the lowest levels of the company.

→ Provide transparency into the performance.

→ Set the expectation levels that are required for the job.

→ Celebrate every small milestone along the way.

7. Instant Feedback

If something goes right, encourage it. If something goes wrong, correct it.

→ By knowing who is accountable for what, we can recognize and reward a job well done. Remember that what gets rewarded gets repeated!

→ Respectively, we can provide the right feedback to the right person to encourage improvements where necessary. Create an environment where people feel safe; instead of being punished for their mistakes, they learn from them.

→ Hold people accountable for outcomes and results, not for following processes. Thus, they have the accountability to change a process that is not working, which then may provide you with the result you are looking for.

> *"If you want to go fast, go alone.*
> *If you want to go far, go together."*
> *−African Proverb*

Accountability is a circle that connects all those involved. As a leader, you are in charge of ensuring your own personal contribution, as well as ensuring the contribution of everyone else. You do this by upholding the top characteristics of leadership: practicing effective communication; having a clear vision; promoting creativity, honesty, and dedication; and through leading by example. Transparent, valuable, and beautiful as a gemstone, accountability is the integrity of your business.

CHAPTER 6
The Transformative Power of Accountability

*"When a man points a finger at someone else,
he should remember that four of his fingers are
pointing at himself."*
–Louis Nizer

What does it look like when a business seizes life by the horns and accepts accountability? What happens when leaders take it upon themselves to uphold accountability and lead by example? What happens in an environment where accountability is tracked, measured, and encouraged? What results do you get when you are able to see all company interactions and outcomes?

I've seen this firsthand many times; you probably have, too. I'll illustrate exactly what I mean by sharing the transformative story of a business that I once helped to resurrect as project manager.

This manufacturing company had been plummeting in business and reputation, and fell into disgrace due to the poor delivery time of its IT department. The delivery times were tragic: two of three enhancements were delivered up to six months late! The late project launches undermined the company's success, destroying its chances of increasing its market share and becoming an industry leader. This failure was furthermore costing the company hundreds of thousands of dollars in canceled advertising programs and lost opportunities.

The company's Chief of Information accepted the monthly reports of operational performance without comment or questioning. He'd divided the company into three departments—Business, Consulting, and Development—and had shrugged off accountability. It wasn't "his" concern. His indifference set the tone for this company's apparent apathy toward its performance.

Of course, there came a point of no return. Eventually, the CIO realized that something had to be done if the company was to stay in business. At that point, I was hired to sort out the mess.

After I was brought in, the first thing I noticed was there were more than a dozen teams involved from two warring departments, and not one of them had discussed accountability. The company's reports were vague and generic, so it was impossible to tell from them which teams were doing well and which were not. The company's failures did not directly impact the IT department, so the folks there weren't complaining. The business department was frustrated, since they only had a 30 to 35 percent chance of getting the system changes they needed. Since no one owned the mistakes and delays, there was always "someone else" who could be blamed. The culture of the organization had withered to the point that failure had become acceptable…even normal. That in itself was lethal to the company's performance.

"Once you accept a problem as yours, you
immediately gain the power to fix it."
–Gordon Tredgold

My first action was to organize the teams and shatter the old "norm" of apathy. I communicated that a 35 percent delivery rate was just not acceptable. I outlined a new way of doing things, including a breakdown of the process where individual teams would be assigned specific responsibilities and would be held account-able for them. I explained how this would allow us to see which teams needed help and guidance, and which teams should be recognized and rewarded. This required changes to the reporting system and the implementation of new milestones and metrics, and demanded a far more transparent and respectful style of communication and cooperation.

We'd be setting a new target—a delivery rate of 70 percent—and tying this into the bonuses. If teams de-livered, they'd be rewarded. This kick-started a bit of healthy competition. At the same time, they realized how team cooperation and interconnection would contribute to the company's overall success—a win-win situation that everyone would benefit from. I was also transparent in showing them that I and the rest of the management team would be paid according to the overall performance, so it was in our best interest to help drive improvements and assist the teams any way we could. We were all in this together, all connected and all accountable in our own ways.

The results? Eye-opening, conducive, and beautiful.

→ **By tracking interactions and progress,** we realized that the development department—which had been typically blamed for delays—was working the hardest and wasn't responsible for the biggest part of the failure. It was actually the design department, since they made the initial commitments to the clients before they understood what was fully involved; they often agreed to deliver things in one month when realistically it would take a minimum of three months.

→ **By sharing accountability,** we reached out to the design department. To solve the delays, we had to make the design team *want* to solve them; the management team incorporated the solutions into the bonus scheme. This ensured that the design team would be rewarded for their successes and that they understood the negative consequences of making commitments the company couldn't keep.

→ **By properly estimating and planning** *before* setting deadlines, the design department learned to control (and meet!) their commitments. We gave them three months to clean their backlogs, re-plan, and recommit to what had previously been guessed at.

→ **By setting precise expectations and a detailed metrics system,** we created new monthly reports that revealed each team's performance, allowing us to hold each of them accountable.

→ **By aligning bonuses,** we were able to ensure the managers *and* the teams maintained their focus. Many businesses make the mistake of rewarding their employees for one task while holding them accountable for another completely different task. Correctly aligning bonuses with the important tasks eliminates mixed messages. People generally feel more accountable for tasks for which they are rewarded.

Once the accountability had been defined, the responsibilities had been delegated, and the incentives and consequences had been outlined, the departments transformed into *real* teams. As the teams began to see their performance skyrocket—once they took control of their success—they were more than happy to be accountable. By the end of the first year, we'd exceeded our goal of 70 percent, and had achieved 81 percent. We'd gone from bankrupt to booming.

Just by incorporating a new culture of accountability, we completely transformed the fate of the company.

The Accountability Lifestyle

"Accountability breeds response-ability."
–Stephen R. Covey

By ensuring that we have the right focus, we ensure that we're aiming at the right target. By instilling accountability, we ensure that we've got the correct person aiming in the correct direction. Remember, when we hold people accountable, **it's important that we are holding them accountable for the outcome, not just for following the process;** otherwise, we run the risk of giving people the opportunity to fail and then blaming the process. As well, by holding our teams accountable for the outcome, we give them more breathing space to solve problems, and the authority to change a process they know isn't working.

I'll share, for example, a strange situation I witnessed last summer when we experienced torrential rain for five days in a row. When the incessant downpour was finally over, the next day dawned sunny and summery at 32° Centigrade (89.6° Fahrenheit). As I drove to work that day, I saw the most bizarre thing. There was the gardener from the council in Wellingtons, standing ankle-deep in floodwater, *watering the plants.* Plants that were also in 4-inch-deep water. When I got to work, I mentioned this to a staff member, who blushed and started to laugh nervously.

"Please don't ask," she said.

This piqued my interest, of course, so I probed a little deeper. It turns out that one of the rules in Germany is that whenever the temperature exceeds 32° Centigrade, the council must water their plants. If he'd had the choice, I'm pretty sure the gardener would not have watered the plants (too much water might even have killed them), but his manager apparently didn't hold him accountable for the outcome. Clearly, the gardener—who either didn't have the authority to question the process or did not want to accept accountability for changing it—was just following protocol. As a result, he watered plants that were practically drowning.

By now, you've probably realized that accountability goes beyond business. It's deeper than personality; it's a matter of character. It's a way of life. And if you're incorporating it for the first time, you'll find that it's a lifestyle change.

*"Good men are bound by conscience and liberated
by accountability."*
–Wes Fessler

You may carry yourself with a more professional con-
duct at work, but you're still the same person wherever you go and at all hours of the day. By embracing
accountability in all your relationships, you'll reap
the rewards in all the areas of your life. Hold yourself
accountable for your contribution to the relationship
when you interact with your spouse, your parents,
your children, your friends, your colleagues, or your
employees. It's an old motto that *how you do something
is how you do anything.*

→ **Involve** others in setting clear, challenging,
exciting, attainable goals.

→ **Give** them the coaching and the authority to
accomplish these goals.

→ **Monitor** progress and provide respectful, accurate
feedback.

→ **Appreciate** everything good; always praise and
recognize all forms of success.

Lead by example. By holding yourself accountable
for your behaviors and their consequences on project
outcomes and company successes, you pave the way
for others to do the same. By holding your employees
accountable for their share of work, you promote responsibility and encourage improvement and progress.
Accountability builds trust and cooperation within
your business, driving your company's performance
to the next level. You'll see the results in the improved

performance, competency, creativity, commitment, satisfaction, and morale.

Communicate to your teams what accountability really is: a golden key opening the gateway to professional and personal gain. By restructuring the company culture around honesty, transparency, and solutions, you will inevitably attain the ability to pinpoint what is and what isn't working, and when, how, and why. You will be able to measure output against expectations, and you'll discover what to change, reward, and improve.

Embrace accountability. Try it on for size. It is the most powerful identifier of success. I promise that it will catapult you to a whole new level of personal and professional performance.

S = Simplicity

"You wanna fly, you got to give up the @#$^ that weighs you down."
–Toni Morrison

Since focus hones in on the "what" and accountability centers around the "who" of the situation, simplicity perfectly answers the "how." It's important to keep our solutions as simple as possible. The simpler we can keep things, the easier it'll be for us to effectively communicate to our team, and the easier it will be for our team to understand and see how it will work. This respective knowledge and confidence is an essential strategy in strengthening our team's belief in the project and objective, thereby drastically increasing the probability of success.

→ How are you going to achieve your goals?

→ What is your approach?

→ Have you chosen the simplest approach possible?

→ Have you explained it simply to your team?

→ Have you instilled belief in your people?

In a world of screaming urgencies and countless choices and responsibility overload, complexity reigns. We feel doomed by the mere thought of how much we *have* to do. Worse, it seems we never actually manage to *do* it all. Our time and our energy are consumed by a fast-paced busyness that ironically does not mirror our low productivity. I'm sure there have been many times—too many times, probably—when you've begun the work day with grand ideas and long-term goals...and realized, twelve hours later, that you've just put out fires all day. Why? There were urgent emails, meetings, phone calls, social media updates, personnel problems, coffee breaks, stacks of documents and bills, and so many more attention-demanding little demons. We succumb to the complexity in our lives as if it is a stun gun that paralyzes us with the overwhelming force of everything that "needs" to get done.

The beauty of it all is that it doesn't have to be that way.

On the fast-track of success, simplicity is your most powerful tool. Simplicity is in the sleek plainness of a runner's outfit, in the focused positioning of his body and mind, and in the uniformity of his unadorned shoes. Simplicity propels you forward down the track with the might of Hermes's winged sandals. This is my gift to you in this section, and my goal: to help you strip off all the complexities that weigh you down, and have you flying above with those winged sandals.

CHAPTER 7
Why We Resist Simplicity

There is a risk in confusing *simple* with *easy*. They are not one and the same. Ask anyone who has tried to lose weight; the formula is so simple (*move more, eat less*), yet that doesn't make it easy. It's often a lot "easier" to get bogged down in complexity. It's usually "easier" to decide *not* to rise to the challenge of simplifying things. It's "easier" to do something the way it's always been done. And of course it's "easier" to think about simplifying something but failing to do so. Then again, on the other end of the spectrum, it may be "easier" to mindlessly go full-out and oversimplify to the point of absurdity.

Simple is also sometimes misunderstood as *stupid*. You can't think of a better or more complex way to do or say something, so you say it simply; you must be stupid, right? After all, the dictionary term of "simpleton" is: "Someone who is not very intelligent or who does not have or show good sense or judgment." We've sadly been conditioned to believe that the more complicated something is, the more intelligent or worthy it must be—when, in fact, the complete opposite is often true!

My terminology of "simple" refers to anything but stupid. "Simple" in this context, is, in the words of da Vinci, "the ultimate sophistication." It is, in the words of George Sand, "the most difficult thing to secure in the world; it is the last limit of experience and the last effort of genius."

The Dangers of Shifting Complexity

"Things which matter most must never be at the mercy of things which matter least."
–Goethe

In 2004, the U.S. Army decided to create a universal camouflage pattern. At first glance, it seemed efficient. The uniform was supposed to blend in with the three basic types of warzone terrains: urban, forested, and desert. Such an ideal uniform would save the country a fortune; the Army wouldn't have to produce a new pattern every time it went to war, and they could scrap the two old patterns (forests and deserts, respectively).[25]

It was an epic failure.

Almost immediately, the idea flunked where it mattered most: out in the battlefield. The pixelated gravely pattern of the "universally blending" uniform did not help soldiers blend in with the desert...or the jungle... or the cities...or anywhere. It could arguably provide coverage for a soldier hiding in a parking lot. But in any

---

[25] http://www.thedailybeast.com/the-hero-project/articles/2013/10/14/the-army-s-5-billion-new-uniform-already-being-replaced.html

other situation, it made the soldiers stick out like sore thumbs...and get shot down like targets.[26, 27]

There are many suggestions as to *why* this was allowed to happen, but several unsubstantiated reports from the media strongly indicate that the army supposedly wanted a more "distinctive" uniform, which would be "cooler" than that of the marines. Ironic, of course, since such a uniform's effectiveness is in its *not* being distinctive. Whatever spurred the creation of this pattern did not take into account the most important factor of all: the safety of the soldiers in the field. The result was an expensive and heartbreaking tragedy, costing billions of dollars and priceless human lives.

> *"Everything should be made as simple as possible,*
> *but not simpler."*
> *—Albert Einstein*

Failure is not something you can brush aside as a mistake. Apart from being too costly in its results, it is too unintelligent. Failures are the mistakes that we won't accept as lessons, mistakes that we continue or amplify. Failure happens when we get knocked down and decide not to get back up.[28]

---

[26] http://www.veteransunited.com/network/army-scrambling-to-replace-the-universal-camouflage-pattern/

[27] http://theweek.com/article/index/238909/the-irresponsibly-stupid-and-dangerous-camouflage-patterns-of-the-us-military

[28] http://activerain.trulia.com/blogsview/1144626/the-difference-between-a-mistake-and-failure-

This legendary fiasco cemented itself as a failure—not a mistake—with the army's lack of damage control. As if the creation and distribution of the failed uniform were not enough, the misaligned focus continued even after the ineffectiveness of the uniform was confirmed. The army failed to recognize the problem, much less confront and fix it; it took years for the army to phase out the uniform. Even a decade later, many continue to wonder why it took so much additional time and money to replace such a tragically ineffective product.

On the surface, the cost of this failure was $5 billion, but the mental, physical, and mortal toll was far greater. Consider the troops who were put at risk, clear targets for the enemy. Consider the ridicule they must have faced within the army, from the other branches of the armed forces and from society in general. Consider the horror of having to explain this to the chief of staff or even the president. At the very best, this failure would be a career killer…definitely not something you'd like to have on your resume.

By trying to simplify the product *too much*, the army regrettably made the process far more complicated. Thanks to misaligned simplification and oversimplification, they set themselves up for failure. In essence, you could also argue that they didn't really simplify anything; they merely shifted the complexity.

The fashion designers of the world must have been pulling out their hair by the roots. Creating one outfit that goes with *everything*?

Darling, no.

The Mantras of Most Managers

> *"It is true intelligence for a man to take a subject*
> *that is mysterious and great in itself and to unfold*
> *and simplify it so that a child can understand it."*
> *–John H. Taylor*

We were meant to live simply. We were meant to communicate simply. The most powerful messages, quotes, books, speakers, mathematical equations, and innovative solutions are the ones that *keep things simple.* If you can keep something simple, you can explain it clearly. If you can explain it clearly, then you understand it. If you can understand it, you can implement it. If you implement it, then you will know success.

As a leader, it is even more crucial that you learn to master simplicity. Given your position and your obligations, you are a figurehead and a face of your organization, and you do lead by example—intentionally or not (hopefully intentionally!). It is your job to ensure that your example is a worthy one.

Yet even though the end result of simplicity is to *make your life easier*, most people resist it. Most managers complain about being overwhelmed, yet few of them are clear-headed enough to let go of what is not necessary. Most managers hide behind an egotistic pride of being "too busy" to deal with other things. Most managers hesitate to let go of obligations, afraid to admit that they've been actually sacrificing productivity for busyness. Most managers are too overloaded with to-do lists to take the time to step back, breathe, and prioritize.

Don't be *most managers.*

→ **Excuse #1: "I'm too busy."**

Exactly. You're too *busy*. You're not too productive. It's important to realize the distinction. Remember the difference between *efficient* and *effective*? I could take my cell phone out and start scrolling through my hundreds of contacts, and I could take a piece of paper and start writing down *all* the names and numbers. It's a back-up plan, right? That makes for a pretty busy day; who knows, it might take even more than one, given all the other busy things that happen to interrupt my flow. Or, I could plug my phone chip into my laptop card reader and copy all the contact information there. It takes about three seconds to complete this alternative back-up plan, and I've been perhaps 300 times more effective *and* efficient. Be busy, but be busy with the things that matter.

→ **Excuse #2: "I like being busy."**

Ah, that is closer to the truth. One of the underlying psychological reasons that we subconsciously *choose* not to simplify our lives is because our culture has transformed the act of "being busy" into a status symbol. Also, we take a certain amount of pride and satisfaction in being needed; if you're needed all day and all night, how much more important can you get? To a certain extent, this behavior is normal. It is innate and universal, springing from one of the most deep-rooted human cravings: the need to be appreciated. On the other hand, we tend to overdo it. Being on numerous committees, micromanaging a dozen people, or not "finding" any time to eat lunch or go to the bathroom has become a source of prestige. You can *still* be appreciated, important, and loved (and probably more so) if you choose to be more productive instead of busy, prioritize more than you multi-task, and keep your bladder happy.

→ **Excuse #3: "I need to do this."**

Do you? Stop and consider if what you're doing really *is* important, or if it's busywork. The Pareto Principle (also called the 80/20 Rule) reveals that roughly 80 percent of our results come from 20 percent of our efforts. Imagine if you could just concentrate on that 20 percent — the 20 percent of customers who bring you profit, the 20 percent of your products that you actually sell, the 20 percent of your sales staff who make those sales, the 20 percent of the hours when your employees are being productive, etc. It's unsettling and disappointing to realize that we might be filling our time with low-value or unnecessary work; as leaders, we *want* to believe that our work is essential and the world will end without us. Sometimes, though, we need a little reminder that the world will go on. We do not run out of time; time runs out of us.

→ **Excuse #4: "A complex problem requires a complex solution."**

We have a tendency to overcomplicate things. How many "experts" do you know who seem to speak a different language when they talk to you about their field of expertise? Have you ever felt that they are purposefully being complex or ambiguous, or showing off? We often suffer from the illusion that complex problems must have complex solutions, and so we start out looking for complexity. Since there's at least one complex solution for every complex problem, and since we find whatever we're looking for, we grasp onto it as the "easy" (yes, easy to come by) solution. A true expert knows how to simplify things and understands the value of doing so. People often resist this challenge, because it means that they might have to admit that *they* don't fully understand their own approach or solution. If you can't explain something, you don't fully understand it. If you can't lower yourself to the comprehension level of your listeners, you're actually no higher than they are.

→ **Excuse #5: "I don't know another way of doing things."**

If you're willing to learn, there's *always* another way of doing things, and it's probably a better way. Doing something one way *just* because it's the standard process is an indicator that this "way" needs investigating. Practically every company that I've worked with has been bogged down by institutionalized bureaucracy, which is always defended by the phrase, *That's the way we've always done it.* Yet they forget this: if you want to get something you've never had, you must do something you've never done.

CHAPTER 8

Ten Ways to Immediately Simplify Your Business

"Simplicity is the ultimate sophistication."
–Leonardo da Vinci

People aren't afraid of hard work if they understand that it *will* lead to success. The belief that they will be successful is what inspires them, yet this belief can only come through that understanding. Given the incessant newsfeed of technology, the senseless hurricane of multi-tasking, and the misaligned priority of what's urgent over what's important, it's easy for your employees to lose their focus, their zest, and their purpose.

Here are ten ways you can save yourself (and your company) valuable time, energy, money, and heartache. Here are ten ways to boost productivity, organization, *and* morale. Here are ten ways to make your own contributions—on a professional and personal scale—more effective, enjoyable, and prosperous.

1 . Reevaluate

Reevaluate the importance of everything. Know how to distinguish between what's important and what's urgent. Especially learn to discern what's urgent and important, and what's urgent but unimportant. If it's not important, try to eliminate it. Simplicity is clarity.

2. Prioritize

A to-do list is basically a wish-list. Scratch it off. Instead, create an MIT (Most Important Tasks) list instead. Set a maximum of THREE things you want to accomplish each day. Decide that if you meet these, your day will have been productive—and not merely busy. Simplicity is order.

3. Cut distractions

As a leader, you should have a greater capability to foresee distractions, especially since you may theoretically have more of them. For example, what are your customers' FAQs? Take the time to write these questions and their answers down; include them in your employees' phone scripts so that your people are prepared. Print these out and post them where your employees can see them; post them on your company's website so clients and prospects can easily access them, and immediately you'll decrease time-consuming inquiry calls. Another example would be to set blocks of time for things that are less important yet often *demand* attention (i.e., let advertising folks know that they can reach you every Wednesday afternoon). Simplicity is straightforward.

4. Use technology shortcuts

Technology is definitely a double-edged sword. The International Association of Business Organizing reports that the average American employee is interrupted by communications technology every ten minutes.[29] We function in a world where we choose to live completely in the spotlight—if you're on Facebook, Twitter, or LinkedIn, you know exactly what I'm talking about—and have our minds squeezed by an electronic leash. I wonder how many times, while reading this chapter, you've stopped to take a call, check your Facebook or Twitter newsfeed, or just check your phone (just in case).

On the other hand, technology is only what you make of it. If you treat it as a resourceful tool, it will function as exactly that. Why not send out mass emails for minor things instead of rounding up everyone for impromptu, prolonged meetings? *Forbes Magazine* broadcasted a Salary.com survey in 2012 showing that employees considered "too many meetings" the #1 time-waster at the office.[30] Find software packages that help keep you on schedule (i.e., TimeClock and TimeCurve), email templates, distance learning programs and software, automated services (electronic tax filing, payrolls, bank statements, etc.), and VoIP systems; you have a world of possibilities at your fingertips. The trick is to navigate

---

[29] http://www.keyorganization.com/time-management-statistics.php

[30] http://www.huffingtonpost.com/amanda-schneider/get-focused-know-your-type_b_3982697.html, http://www.forbes.com/sites/susanadams/2013/03/21/how-we-waste-time-at-work/

this world wisely, and not get killed by its wild animals and freak storms. Simplicity is resourceful.

5. Cost reduction vs. work reduction[31]

Cost reduction means that you're trying to reduce your costs in order to increase profits; these decisions affect costs. Most employers begin by analyzing their expenses and cutting out excess costs (space, vehicles, utilities, etc.). Cost-cutting may be geared toward a specific department or product (i.e., marketing, design, production, raw materials), or focused geographically (closing or selling a branch of the company that isn't profitable), or geared toward a specific target market that is more trouble than it is worth (remember the 80/20 Principle!). Work reduction means that you're trying to reduce the amount of work you're doing, whether by eliminating, minimizing, or delegating certain tasks. This can affect cost, time, and money. Simplicity is purposeful.

> "Besides the noble art of getting things done, there is the noble art of leaving things undone. The wisdom of life consists in the elimination of non-essentials."
> –Lin Yutang

6. Hire strategically

It's a fact that the quality and quantity of your life and mine are determined by the people we surround ourselves with. Ronald Reagan has remained in history as

---

[31] http://humanresources.about.com/od/layoffsanddownsizing/bb/cut_workforce.htm

one of America's smartest presidents—not because of his own high intelligence, but because he had the brains and charisma to surround himself with a Cabinet of more intelligent people. Andrew Carnegie, a king of the steel industry, followed the same dictum. As a manager and leader, you have an incredible advantage in that you have a lot of power in choosing with whom you'll interact professionally. For your sake and for the sake of your business, it is imperative that you hire people strategically. When you consider someone for your team, there are specific things you should take into account, depending on your own vision and desires for the business's success, both within and beyond the company walls. Employee turnover should be a premeditated decision and a long-term investment, not a sudden or unwanted turn of events.

Know what you want, and why. Determine the professional requirements and standards you have for the position. Don't cut corners; the more time and energy you invest in finding the right people, the less you'll have to worry about their inadequacy later. Consider what your candidate can bring to the table. You have to differentiate between what is essential and what is preferable. Learn to glean the necessary information from interviews, verify credentials, and don't underestimate personality traits. How does this person fit with your own personality as a leader, and how would he or she meld with the rest of the company? Create a team that compliments its strengths and overcomes its weaknesses.

Simplicity is insightful.

7. Focus on the 20 percent

Quite simply, less can literally mean more.

→ Do the 20 percent of the work that results in 80 percent of your success. How many of those tasks are necessary or lead you toward your goal? How many can be delegated, outsourced, or even eliminated?

→ Focus on the 20 percent of your clients who provide 80 percent of your profits. Fire the rest; use the extra time to concentrate on your more valuable clients—and outline their top traits so that you'll be able to reel in more clients like them.

→ Recognize and reward the 20 percent of the employees who bring in 80 percent of the sales (or ensure 80 percent of customer satisfaction). Identify who generates the most success and encourage this.

→ Realize what 20 percent of people are the cause of 80 percent of your interruptions.

→ Pinpoint what 20 percent of working hours generate 80 percent of the company's output.

→ Do the math. If you focus on the 20 percent that gets you 80 percent of the results with 100 percent of your effort, you'll multiply your success. 5 x 20 percent effort could equal 5 x 80 percent output (which equals 400 percent!).

And so forth. Focus on the 20 percent that matters and do something about it. Simplicity is discerning.

8. Eliminate the middleman

Eliminating the middleman might seem a little scary, but it's usually a financial win-win for both ends (seller and buyer) by crossing out an expensive yet often unnecessary distribution step. There are times when a middleman may save you considerable time and resources—electronic bills are a great "middleman" between you and the bank, so you don't have to actually drag yourself to the actual bank every time. However, by taking on the role yourself, you can:

→ Gain control over the approaches, negotiations, and contracts initiated or accepted by your company.

→ Cultivate one-on-one relationships with your own suppliers and customers, and expose yourself to the latest projects, products, and prospects in the field.

→ Cut costs by pocketing the intermediary's percentage of the deal.

Simplicity is independent.

9. Outsource and delegate

In light of all the tasks and projects that must be tackled in the business, you can categorize them all into two basic groups: low-value activities (activities that keep you busy but don't result in high productivity) and high-value activities (activities that produce your most important outcomes). The most successful entrepreneurs are excellent delegators. Part of this is in knowing what tasks to delegate to others: chiefly, tasks that are low-value for you, allowing you to spend that time on high-value tasks instead. Another part is in your understanding of outsourcing tools and solutions. Get online to send your invoices, reminders, and bills, and to find expert freelancers in any time zone and in any language to virtually assist you in anything.

1. Know what you want to delegate. Identify the win-win-win situation (figure out how you, the person to whom you delegate the task, and the overall company all win).

2. Know who you want to delegate it to. By determining that person's "win" in the situation and conveying it, you'll have many more people who will accept and even desire your delegation.

3. Take advantage of your "win": use that extra time, money, or energy to the best of your advantage.

Keep your systems simple, team-oriented, and streamlined. Simplicity is interconnected.

10. Unplug

Believe it or not, there's a "National Simplify Your Life Week" in America, beginning each August 1. Imagine our need to unplug, unwind, and rebalance ourselves; we've wound up making life so busy, complex, and overwhelmingly out of hand, that we need a *national holiday reminder* to set things straight. We think of ourselves as the most stressed-out, personality-disorder-diagnosed, overeating, and overworked generation to date, yet there isn't a saber-tooth tiger in sight. We forget what our ancestors knew and practiced, without modern-day distractions that tend to strip us of our serenity, harmony, and humanity.

→ Clear the clutter. Organize your workspace, your home, your relationships, and your mind. Eliminate what doesn't matter. Focus on what matters.

→ Embrace nature. Not just for productivity or creativity's sake (studies show that a brief excursion into the wild boosts creativity by 50 percent), but for your own health and longevity. A brief walk outside lowers your risk for all diseases, strengthens your muscles and heart, increases circulation and energy, and uplifts your mood.

→ Cut your commute. Do you spend half your day stuck in traffic or flying across the country for business meetings? Take advantage of those hours differently by trying alternatives like video conferences or working from home.

It's important to create boundaries. Set aside ten minutes for personal calls. Set aside ten minutes a day for headline browsing and Facebook. Spend at least two hours doing something fun with the family before you burn some late-night oil. Simplicity is balance.

"We have lost contact with reality, the simplicity
of life."
–Paolo Coelho

CHAPTER 9

The Art of Simplification

"Life is really simple, but we insist on making it complicated."
–Confucius

Remember that your teams will only be inspired when they have the belief that they will succeed. This belief is something you instill in them through their *understanding*. Understanding emerges after simplification. When we simplify something, it allows us to increase our focus and our dedication; understanding something makes us happy.

I remember working for a leading electrical company. During a period of deregulation, we needed to design a new billing system. The specification of the system took nine months to write and was several volumes thick. Although the project was delivered on time, it was over our budget, overly complex, and didn't even fully meet the needs of the customer. We sat there facing over 1,000 pages—scary—of detailed requirements from the business.

When it was time to build the second phase of the system, I was tasked with that requirement analysis. I arranged a meeting with the new billing manager, who told me, "Look, billing is very, very simple. I have three key requirements: prompt, accurate meter readings; prompt, accurate invoices; and prompt payment of the invoices."

I was dumbfounded. He'd simplified it so beautifully, and yet nowhere in our 1,000-page requirements was this mentioned.

I grabbed onto this simplicity. Once it was crystal-clear to me what he wanted and what was important, I could clearly understand the business's needs. As we moved to upgrade the system, we created posters and printed these three key requirements on the wall. We used them as a guide to ensure that we designed the system that was needed; they were our cornerstone for any decision making regarding prioritization. This time, we excitedly delivered the project on time and within budget.

Every time we tackled a new feature or idea for the system, we challenged it against our three standards:

→ **Did it increase the accuracy or promptness of the meter reading?**

→ **Did it improve the accuracy or promptness of the invoicing?**

→ **Did it help to get the invoices paid on time?**

If not, we either discarded it or placed it aside for a later release date. I explained to the billing manager how his conversation with me had really helped the team focus on what was important. I dug a little deeper, asking why he'd chosen these as the most critical requirements. He replied that prompt payment was one way to increase company profits; the company had to pay interest on the money that it borrowed in order to purchase the electricity that it then sold to the customers. The longer the customers took to pay, the more interest the company was forced to pay to provide the service. He continued with an analysis of why decreasing our days outstanding was a significant goal, and then he dove into the intricacies of short-term lending.

This conversation was very interesting but also quite complex. I'm sure that if this hour-long talk had been printed out, paragraphs and paragraphs of it, to tack up on the wall to serve as our guideline requirements, the project would have been more likely to overrun; we'd have focused on reducing days outstanding. We wouldn't have been able to pinpoint the three standards that directly correlated to our success. Most of all, it was a matter of reevaluating, prioritizing, and focusing on the 20 percent. It was a matter of simplification and communication, which spring from the heart of effective leadership. By fusing the principles of Focus and Simplicity—first focusing and then simplifying—we triumphed.

Remember…

→ **Reevaluate**

→ **Prioritize**

→ **Cut distractions**

→ **Use technology shortcuts**

→ **Reduce costs and work accordingly**

→ **Hire strategically**

→ **Focus on the 20 percent**

→ **Eliminate the middleman**

→ **Outsource and delegate**

→ **Unplug**

As a leader, it is your job to ensure that you are reducing complexity. Keep things as simple as possible. Keep your eyes on the prize. Give up whatever is weighing your company down. This is the fast-track to success, but I promise you that you will not be running toward the finish line of goal after goal after goal.

Because why run when you can fly?

T = Transparency

"Honesty is the first chapter in the book of wisdom."
–Thomas Jefferson

Now that we've got focus, accountability, and simplicity covered, it's time to place the final piece of the puzzle: transparency. We've answered "what," "who," and "how"…but what about "where"? Focus, accountability, and simplicity may seem pretty self-explanatory if you scratch the surface; transparency is a bit more ambiguous. Transparency is about marking progress and tracking time. It's about clarity; for instance, knowing that a marathon is 1,000 kilometers in terms of training, and not 42.2 (26.2 miles). It is our honesty about both our progress and our capability. When I speak of transparency, I am actually referring to the blend of truth and knowledge of where we really are, what our real performance is, and what we need to do in order to succeed.

→ **How far have you come toward your goals and objectives?**

→ **How far do you still need to go in order to achieve success?**

Regardless of what industry you're dealing with, *transparency* means an honest, timely, and authentic way of doing business. It means integrity and honesty: clear, accurate, unhidden data, based on facts and delivered in a timely manner. It is truth upheld by accountability, and fostered by respect and cooperation. Transparency is the consciousness of where you stand, the illumination of a map that will show where you need to go next.

CHAPTER 10

How You Do Anything is How You Do Everything

There are actually a number of credible studies that reveal that all humans have an innate proclivity to lie. Whether we are consciously trying to deceive someone, whether we are trying to contain a situation with a "white lie," or whether we're simply adding some sauce to our version of the story, some findings argue that 60 percent of us can't go ten minutes into a conversation without lying.[32] A study in the UK estimated that men lie six times a day (twice as much as women) to their partners, bosses, and colleagues.

The most common fib? Anything along the lines of "nothing's wrong; I'm fine."[33]

---

[32] http://mentalfloss.com/article/30609/60-people-cant-go-10-minutes-without-lying

[33] http://edition.cnn.com/2010/WORLD/europe/05/20/britain.lies.study/index.html

This isn't to say that we're all compulsive liars or conniving cutthroats who seek to torment the people around us. A study from University of Toronto claims that becoming a liar (usually a feat decently accomplished by the age of four) is "an important developmental milestone" and "an integral part of healthy brain development."[34] Apparently it proves the development of our essential "theory of mind"—the consciousness that there are beliefs, desires, and intentions beyond one's own—which helps us interact, manipulate, or empathize with other the people.

While the ability to lie may indicate healthy mental development, the *choice* to lie is a different story altogether. There are just as many studies—and I'm sure we both can dig up some personal anecdotes—that prove how lying hurts both the liar and those who are directly or indirectly affected by the lie. Lies shatter trust and faith, which make up the foundation of all stable personal and professional relationships. On a physical level, lying is also stressful, emotionally draining, and decreases our physical and mental health. Of course, lies also deter the progress of your projects. If problems exist, they should be detected, shared, and analyzed as soon as possible. We need to be honest in order to give people the opportunity to fix problems and not just mourn them.

How transparent you are in both your personal and professional spheres is a choice that impacts everything you do and everyone with whom you interact. Obviously, your behavior, stemming from who you are in character, is going to be projected in all situations. It's impossible to

---

34   http://mentalfloss.com/article/30609/60-people-cant-go-10-minutes-without-lying

be a dictator at work and encourage a democracy at home, or vice versa. You are one person—a richly and intriguingly multifaceted, wonderful person, yet still one person.

How you do anything is generally how you do everything.

In business, it's crucial that we have an accurate and clear understanding of the costs and benefits of our actions. Failing to judge, analyze, and balance these factors can cost you very dearly; I recall one business project that haunts me to this day. What had originally seemed a healthy investment had ended up as a venture that would cost us $100 million with an annual benefit of $1 million. Unfortunately, this was something we'd realized *after* hitting the $70 million mark, at which point it was too late to effectively backtrack. If we'd been transparent in our expectations and projections from the very beginning, this could have been avoided; the project would have been canceled before even a dollar had been spent, let alone $70 million!

> *"A lack of transparency results in distrust and a*
> *deep sense of insecurity."*
> —Dalai Lama

In fact, a number of studies have revealed that the average project ends up costing at least *three times* more than the original estimate. Yet while it's impossible to set things in stone, or to estimate things with 100 percent accuracy, it *is* possible to be effectively proactive, competent, and ready. At the beginning of a project, most people choose to see only the tip of the iceberg. It's extremely dangerous navigating the waters if you can only see the tip. On the other hand, having full transparency enables us to see beneath the surface and judge the entire length and width of the iceberg. We have a clear understanding of everything that's involved and what is needed in order for us to succeed. We make decisions based on that information. Remember that your decisions are only as sound as the information you base them upon.

I'm not telling you anything you don't know; I merely hope to remind you of things you may often forget. If you cultivate and practice honesty, integrity, and respectfulness at home, you will bring these traits to your work environment, and vice versa. In a business, your professional transparency (or lack thereof) is widely regarded as a projection of your personal reputation.

As a leader, remember that you are the figurehead—the face—of your business; it should come as no surprise that your business's authenticity inevitably reflects your *own* authenticity. You are your business's face, and whether you are clean or whether you are masked can make all the difference in the world.

The GPS of Your Business

Do you have a GPS in your car? If so, you're aware of what an invaluable instrument it can be. A GPS gives you great peace of mind because it ensures a clear route. You know how long it'll take to get from A to B, and you know exactly where you are at any given time. You even know your expected time of arrival. If you need to be somewhere, like the office or the airport, by 8 a.m., and your GPS forecasts a destination time of 8:30 a.m., you know you need to stop dawdling. It's wisest to check your GPS before you even begin. If it estimates the journey will take an hour, plan for extra time on the road in case of emergencies or traffic. While you're driving, you get constant feedback about your whereabouts, about how far you've come, and about how far you've yet to go.

Life goes on without a GPS, of course. But it's more of a struggle. You create more work for yourself; you set up your own obstacles and roadblocks by your ignorance. That would be okay if you know the area or if you don't mind being stuck in traffic for hours and hours. If not, however, you could end up late, lost, or frustrated. In the worst case, you won't know where you are, where you need to go, or how long it'll take you to get there. It's a recipe for failure—and one you could have easily avoided! Remember the old adage: *fail to plan, and plan to fail.*

Transparency is the GPS of the business world.

Since a large part of transparency deals with understanding where we are and tracking our progress, you must ensure that you have some sort of measuring stick. In the sports world, competition requires *and* ensures the use of clear, accurate measurement tools. In soccer games, for instance, we keep score using a league table, which lists the competitors in a league and ranks them based on that season's performance. It's an accurate comparison chart that is updated after each and every game. So a team could argue they played the best, or they were unlucky, or they are the most favored team, but no one can argue with the results! Numbers talk; the results speak for themselves. Whether the teams like them or not, the results are the true reflection of their performance. The team that wins first place at the end of the season is the team that will be crowned champion.

Keeping track of where we are—realistically, in an accurate and timely fashion—is imperative to our success. In the business world, EVM is one such tool; you could think of it as the GPS of complex projects. Earned Value Measurement (or Earned Value Project/Performance Measurement) is a project management technique used to objectively quantify performance and progress, combining measurements of the scope, schedule, and cost of the project. As such, it can be scaled to fit any project in terms of size and complexity, and provides extremely accurate measurements for individual factors or combinations (such as budget spent vs. progress, or time spent vs. budget).

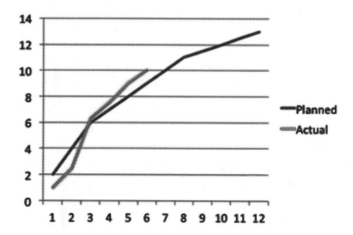

Alternatively and more simply, you can create your own chart, pitting actual performance against planned performance. It doesn't matter if your preference is for line graphs or bar charts; the most important point is to have such a chart, and monitor it. In a diagram like the one below, you'd be able to assess where you are, judge whether or not you're on track, and see where you need to change your approach.

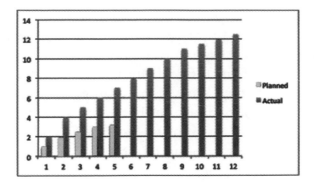

Then there are the Hockey Stick Charts.[35] I see these very often when reviewing projects. This type of chart is a progress chart that shows little to no progress during the project's early stages, yet reveals a drastic increase in the later stages of the project, resulting in ultimate success. It's important to understand the event that causes this significant boost in performance. The Hockey Stick Effect—projecting a chart like this from the beginning, and predicting such progress—is usually wishful thinking on the manager's part. Realistically, this rarely happens. By having a culture of transparency, we help ourselves stay on track.

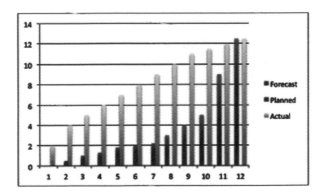

---

[35] http://en.wikipedia.org/wiki/Hockey_stick_graph

In one of the companies I was involved in, I'd tackled a two-year project that was basically a wide-spanning and very difficult transformational program. When we were about halfway through, the team's motivation and belief began to flag. We were receiving a lot of criticism from some of our colleagues in the business; it felt like we'd never get to the light at the tunnel's end. Winston Churchill's quote became an anthem: *"If you're going through hell, keep going."*

I realized that, if I wanted to be an effective leader and rouse the team, I needed to do a better job of my job, and that included showing people how far they'd come and how much they'd accomplished. My job wasn't just to point the way. It was just as important to prove to them how much they'd already achieved, to praise them for their great effort, and to inspire them to continue pushing through.

I set up a meeting with the entire leadership team of approximately fifty leaders, armed with my direct reports and their direct reports, and worked to re-motivate them. To work with as much transparency as possible, I ensured that we had plenty of metrics available to us, and we carefully outlined our key performance indicators. I began the presentation by highlighting how tough the project was and how, if we had to do it all over again, I might have chosen to be a little less ambitious; I apologized for my aggressive goal-setting.

The team fully agreed.

I continued with this tone throughout the presentation, influencing my audience's mood. The statistics, once we finally laid our cards on the table, made them even happier. The data showed that although we were 50 percent of the way through the program, we'd achieved 60 percent of the overall results, and our performance was higher than we'd predicted for this stage. These findings allowed me to change my tone to mirror the figure, and the mood tangibly shifted. Once we had proof of our success and our progress, we allowed ourselves to feel hope, even pride. We re-immersed ourselves in the belief that we would be successful, and that we would exceed all of our goals.

I wrapped up the meeting by telling my team how proud I was of them; that they'd accepted and were tackling extremely aggressive goals; that they'd allowed me to really challenge them and push them beyond their comfort zone. I told them that, despite this all, we were ahead of schedule and on the brink of major success. The leadership team left the meeting visibly motivated and went on to inspire their own teams by passing on these messages.

By choosing transparency and implementing truth and knowledge, we accomplished what others had believed to be impossible.

CHAPTER 11

Teetering on the Tightrope of Transparency

"I always say be humble but be firm. Humility and openness are the keys to success without compromising your beliefs."
–George Hickenlooper

You're balancing between secrecy and oversharing; the line is actually quite fine. Where's the border between refreshing honesty and Big Brother surveillance? Can you discern it? As a leader, you need to.

If you do it well, it will be the best thing you've ever done for your business.

Here are basic guidelines to keep in mind while you work to maintain your balance, prevent oversharing, and protect yourself, your team, and your business:

→ **Follow the policy of *less is more*.** Share relevant information that is appropriate to your audience.

→ **Choose your outlets wisely.** Remember that, most of the time, images and videos can stir people's emotions quicker and more powerfully than words.

→ **Don't blur the lines** between the professional and personal spheres of your life.

→ **Lead by example and communicate these principles** to your employees and teams; teach them to embrace a culture of transparency without oversharing.

→ Ensure that your information mirrors the three key characteristics of transparency. **Ask yourself:**

o **Is it authentic?**

o **Is it timely?**

o **Is it consistent?**

You can increase transparency with review meetings and effective communication by monitoring and assessing progress, and by holding yourself and your team accountable. You can use budget reports, sales P&L reports, operation performance statistics, and so forth. With the right granularity of data, you can best identify what's working and what isn't, while keeping everyone onboard and motivated.

You can begin today, easily implementing transparency and immediately reaping the benefits. Here are just a handful of ideas…

→ When Hiring

Share your concerns and ask for those of your interviewees. It not only establishes a baseline of trust and respect, but also helps you manage expectations and pinpoint deal-breakers. As in any budding relationship, if you're straightforward and clean about who you are and what you're looking for, you automatically boost your chances of finding it.

→ When Involving

Clear communication promotes clear results. Be clear and transparent about what you want, but also be clear and transparent about how you convey this to your people. Maintaining open and honest communication helps weed out gossip or anxiety, and helps boost morale, job satisfaction, and company loyalty.

→ When Reviewing

Track and measure performance and progress in order to stay aligned with your goals and focused on success. If your teams aren't meeting the agreed-upon expectations and deadlines, deal with it by bringing that matter to their attention and by brainstorming solutions.

→ When Revising or Replacing

It's important that employees know what they're doing right or wrong. Enforce the right things by encouraging them; minimize the wrong things by acknowledging and dealing with them. If things don't improve, you might have to cut the cord and let someone go. They should know why.

→ When Prospecting, Promoting, and Performing

The most basic rule of thumb? Be transparent from the beginning and in all things. This involves your deals with external forces—prospects, clients, suppliers, the competition, etc.—and make sure your staff is somehow involved. Employees are more likely to trust you if you are open with them. Customer service also enjoys a big boost if you are looking to deal with prospects and clients in a clean way.

→ Start Small

The folks at Buffer suggest something as simple as bulk emailing. They suggest creating a CC list for every email between two or more people and any team. Start by sharing something that isn't critical and see how it feels, then build from there. You'll find some incredible benefits.

→ Start Immediately

Practice "due diligence," which basically means: investigate your investment before you invest! In a nutshell, if you're making cookies for other people, you need to know how many people you're expecting to feed. If you want to cater to 100 people, and you've only got a half-cup of flour, you're not going to pull through at this party. If you don't know what you're up against before you begin, you won't have the ability to effectively plan anything...and you'll be very disappointed when a hundred people show up to eat ten cookies. (Needless to say, so will they.)

→ Start With What You Already Have

Whether you've realized it or not, you have plenty of data—sales reports, cost reports, revenue reports, stock tables, and so forth—already available to you, with which you can monitor and track performance. The trick is in knowing how to leverage this data to create an accurate and automated performance marker, which will allow you to most effectively steer your company.

The Currency of Leadership

> *"I'd always rather err on the side of openness.*
> *But there's a difference between optimum and*
> *maximum openness, and fixing that boundary is*
> *a judgment call. The art of leadership is knowing*
> *how much information you're going to pass on."*
> *–Warren Bennis*

The alternative of transparency is confusion, misalignment, and uncertainty. Confusion leads to miscommunication; misalignment results in poor performance and wrong outcomes; and uncertainty becomes fear and resentment. The talent management company ClearCompany.com compiled data revealing the dangers. No matter what you call it—blindness, a broken GPS, or a toxic company culture—the results are as follows:

- → **5.9 percent:** the number of companies that daily communicate their goals.

- → **10 percent:** how much of the company's alignment is visible to the average CEO.

→ **14 percent:** the number of companies whose workers understand the company's strategy, goals, and direction.

→ **44 percent:** the number of workers who can't specifically name the company goals (even if they're familiar with them).

→ **Less than 50 percent:** how many companies are at least 80 percent aligned with their goals.

→ **57 percent:** the amount of business leaders who see misalignment during goal cascading as a big challenge.

→ **60 percent:** the number of employees who complain about insufficient feedback from upper management.

→ **70 percent:** the number of employees who are disengaged on the job.

→ **$350+ billion:** what the aforementioned disengagement is costing businesses.[36]

On the flipside, here's what immediately begins to happen when we start to clear the air by incorporating a culture of transparency:

→ **Aligned work.**

→ **More productive teams.**

→ **Empowered and happier employees.**

→ **Faster onboarding.**

→ **Improved communications.**

---

[36] http://theundercoverrecruiter.com/roadmap-greater-company-transparency-infographic/

Businesses are 50 percent more likely to enjoy lower employee turnover if they practice effective communication.[37] There's an increase of highly engaged employees who understand the importance of their contributions to the company's success, and companies with highly-engaged employees enjoy 22 percent greater productivity.[38]

The LMX (Leader-Member Exchange) Model proposes that the quality of relationships between leaders and members reflects the authenticity of their mutual transactions. Members feel better about and more connected to their leaders when they view them as ethical, honest, consistent, communicative, and fair. This works best if the viewpoint is mutual. If their mutual trust and respect is lacking, the quality of the personal relationship and the commitment to the professional relationship is drastically reduced. Thus, it is first and foremost the leader's job—your job—to be as honest, fair, and ethical as possible in all your professional transactions. It is your job to connect with your members and to do everything in your power to avoid alienating them.

"I think the currency of leadership is transparency. You've got to be truthful. I don't think you should be vulnerable every day, but there are moments where you've got to share your soul and conscience with people and show them who you are, and not be afraid of it."
–Howard Schultz

---

[37] http://www.businessperform.com/workplace-communication/poor-communication-costs.html

[38] http://www.imagemakersintl.com/blog/archives/02-2014

Yet transparency can be a tough tightrope to walk. Utter transparency is not always achievable—or beneficial. There is such a thing as TMI (too much information)! Information overload can cause mental asphyxia, which makes us stressed, overwhelmed, and unable to focus or concentrate. This causes mistakes, leeches valuable brain power, or simply wastes time. Being *too* transparent—intentionally or not—almost always backfires.

These days, all you have to do is log into a social media network to get an idea. Take examples such as the story of twenty-three-year-old Carly McKinney, a high school teacher who narrated the more personal aspects of her life on social media (half-naked photos, pictures and status updates about drug use, etc.).[39] She was promptly "caught"—and fired, of course—when the school administration found her on the Internet (it wasn't hard). Statistics show that this generation of "millennials" does, in general, have a penchant for oversharing, further blurring the lines between their personal and professional lives. For many people, this lack of boundaries has cost them their jobs, their relationships, and their reputations.

The former Vice President of Hewlett-Packard, Scott McClellan, unintentionally gave his competitors a peek at some very valuable information when he cited, on his LinkedIn profile, some undisclosed data about the

---

[39] http://www.capitalbay.com/latest-news1/302505-carly-mckinney-high-school-teacher-23-tweeted-nude-photos-of-herself-called-her-students-jail-bait-and-talked-about-getting-high.html

company's cloud-computing services.[40] The information was quickly pulled down, but the damage from the leak was done. A Forrester Research survey says that 82 percent of 150+ companies that monitor social media reportedly use this information for competitive intelligence.[41] Monitoring the competitor is a historical concept, but the methods have become plentiful, accessible, and very user-friendly.

In a glass house, surveillance, plagiarism, and stalking have never been easier.

---

[40] http://www.bloomberg.com/news/2011-09-20/hewlett-packard-executive-proves-hazard-of-sharing-linkedin-profiles-tech.html

[41] http://www.salesbenchmarkindex.com/bid/97422/3-Steps-to-Combining-Social-Media-Competitive-Intelligence

CHAPTER 12

Renovating Your Business: A Glass-Walled Mind-set of Trust

"Transparency is not the same as looking straight through a building. It's not just a physical idea; it's also an intellectual one."
—Helmut Jahn

Ten Immediate Benefits of Transparency

Buffer is a social media-sharing company that has benefitted stupendously from a policy of groundbreaking transparency, and they proudly broadcast this fact, encouraging others to do the same. When they announced job openings in December 2013, they also decided to reveal their pay structure to the world. They also uphold their value of transparency by publically updating revenues, progress reports, and self-improvement mission statements. Predictably, their unorthodox policy turned heads. Shortly afterward, they were bombarded with resumes (more than 1,000 in a month) and enjoyed a dramatic increase in candidate quality.[42]

Transparency is a policy that breeds trust across the board, and ensures far more solid transactions. At the same time, it gives you extra leverage by being the road less traveled. Perhaps most importantly of all, it could save the skin of your company.

At the start of 2014, McDonald's was attacked by a rumor (and a photo on the Internet that allegedly supported this accusation) that their Chicken McNuggets were made of "pink slime." Not only was pink slime (or what the meat industry calls "lean finely textured beef") a highly controversial product in and of itself, but McDonald's promised to stop using it after a campaign by celebrity chef Jamie Oliver.

McDonald's immediately responded to this attack with a public statement countering the image and allegation. McDonald's Canada also created a brief but very powerful documentary that went behind the scenes and captured the whole supply chain and manufacturing process. It was very well received, showing a raw, gross but truthful reality. The video was commended for showcasing the company's fearless transparency and, as a result, for clearing the air.[43]

---

[42]   http://qz.com/169147/applications-have-doubled-to-the-company-that-discloses-its-salaries/#/h/42900,3/

[43]   https://www.linkedin.com/today/post/article/20140325214716-758871-why-transparency-and-authenticity-wins

This is just one example among a myriad of others, showing how transparency can serve as the most formidable armor. If you are clean and someone throws mud at you—rumors, hearsay, innuendos, etc.—that mud will have nothing to stick to; it'll just fall back down upon your attacker's face.

> *"Transparency, honesty, kindness, good stewardship, even humor, work in businesses at all times."*
> –John Gerzema

Here's the golden ticket: it's a win-win situation. Good ethics *and* good business.

Below, I have outlined ten key benefits of transparency.

1. **A happier workplace.** Management transparency is actually the leading factor in gauging employee satisfaction. This includes boosted morale, job satisfaction, and...

2. **Increased company loyalty**, from within and beyond the company—from employees to shareholders to clients to suppliers.

3. **Clarified expectations and roles.** Managerial expectations are much better conveyed; employee roles are more easily understood. As a result...

4. **Increased efficiency and productivity.** The flow of information is like oxygen in the body's central nervous system. Which also means...

5. **Higher profit.** And, obviously...

6. **Happier shareholders and regulators.**

7. **Stronger company values** (especially resulting from clearly and consistently communicating a company's vision, mission, and values).

8. **A better reputation**. Transparency breeds trust.

9. **Control**. I overhead the Internet being called "the dishwasher of society." It makes sense, if you think about it. In a way it is just that, an anarchic sea of information and misinformation, where exposure happens at the click of a mouse. The more transparent you are, the less you have to hide. There is less of a void for others to fill with misinformation. Transparency fosters credibility, enabling you to control your reputation to whatever extent possible.

10. **Gain without pain**. Transparency is a little-to-no-cost initiative with huge payoffs, making it your best investment.

Running Blind

On November 9, 2014, I ran my fourth marathon in Athens, following the footsteps of the original marathoner. As I had during my prior marathons, I set a goal of breaking my personal record. My previous scores were 5:12, 5:02, and 5:12 again. This time I wanted to break that time barrier. I wanted to complete the marathon in less than 5 hours.

I knew that to do this, I'd have to run at an average of 7 kilometers/minute. Athens is known to be a very tough course; most of the people I knew were planning to run conservatively. The going gets steep. It's relatively flat for the first 10 kilometers, it's pretty much uphill from kilometer 10 to 32, and then it slopes downhill for the remainder of the journey until it culminates in the breathtaking Olympic stadium. I also had to take into account the fact that people always run a little more than the full 42.2 kilometers; just dodging and weaving around other runners—not to mention stopping for drinks and bathroom breaks—usually results in running up to a full extra kilometer.

The day of the race dawned a bit warmer than most of us expected. At the start, it was 18 degrees Centigrade (64° Fahrenheit), climbing up to 26.6° by midday. I prefer to run in cooler temperatures, but the heat wouldn't be stopping me. I was a man on a mission. I clung to my dream of finishing the marathon in less than five hours.

My training had gone well. I'd done quite a bit of traveling before the marathon, disrupting my training plan and ensuring that I didn't over-train as I'd once done in a previous marathon. My plan was to run the first 10 kilometers at 6:30 minutes/kilometer, pace myself at 7 minutes/kilometer going uphill, and then pick up some speed during the final 10 kilometers. When I tackle long distances, over 20 kilometers, I typically use the Jeff Galloway method, switching between walking and running in order to conserve energy and de-stress muscles. I'd seen major improvements in the past by alternating between 3-minute runs and 1-minute walks.

So I'd be okay, right?

On that summery November day in Greece, the race began. The first 10 kilometers breezed by; I felt strong, and my application showed that I was right on schedule. Then the hills reared up before us. My pace slowed, and I needed to keep reminding myself that it was okay because it was the plan. The roughest terrain appeared between the 25-kilometer and 32-kilometer marks, where my average was 8 minutes/kilometer. I started to get concerned, but remembered that the ground would soon begin to slope down.

Until that point, I was using the Nike+ application on my phone as my guide. It indicated when to switch from running to walking, it informed me about the distance and my average speed, and provided all the transparency I needed in order to align myself with timely progress. As I crossed the crest of the hill at the 32-kilometer mark, I was delighted to see the ground curving downhill. I crossed the 34-kilometer signpost at exactly the 4-hour mark. My phone indicated that I had exactly 8.2 kilometers left to run, which meant that I just needed to average 7:18 minutes/kilometer for the remaining journey. Definitely doable!

Then my iPhone died on me.

I don't know if the heat or the jarring run was to blame. But I was devoid of technology and running blind. I could no longer estimate my average speed or measure the run-walk distances. I tried to keep count in my head, but my body was exhausted. I also couldn't judge distance that well since I was suddenly running downhill. The ratios were important to me, so I tried to estimate 3- and 1-minute marks as best as I could.

I focused on the positive. The crowds were thickening, their shouts and yelling spurring us on. The downhill slope was supportive. I could hear celebratory music in the distance. And finally, up ahead, I saw the magnificent stadium glistening in the noonday sun. Propelled by the magical beauty and energy of my surroundings,

I found myself sprinting the last 200 meters to the finish line.

Had I broken my 5-hour barrier? Had I achieved a personal best?

It turns out I'd run a personal best, completing the marathon in 5:00:09. Everyone congratulated me; this marathon had been so difficult, there were many people who had not finished the course. Nevertheless, I was disappointed. I'd missed my personal dream of breaking the 5-hour record in Athens by *9 measly seconds.*

Personally, it was a reminder of the power of transparency. I realized that I'd probably lost time by walking longer than I should have during those final 10 kilometers. If I'd had the transparency provided by my phone, I'm sure I would have made it in time. Transparency allows us to know exactly where we are and what we need to do in order to be successful. Without it, we are running blind. When we run blind, we can't see well enough to snatch victory from the jaws of defeat.

Harder, Better, Faster, Stronger

> *"Truth never damages a cause that is just."*
> *—Mahatma Gandhi*

Transparency is simple, but it's not easy. It can seem scary. It can even seem silly; who *wants* to air their dirty laundry? But the only way you'll take that laundry down and wash it—and then hang it up again for the world to see, this time clean and smelling heavenly—is by noticing it and acknowledging its dirtiness in the first place...even if that means putting it on display for others so that you're forced to see it yourself.

Perhaps you've been tempted to question the benefit of—or even, the *need* for—transparency. In our fast-paced world, it sometimes seems that "Survival of the Fittest" has been reduced to an ugly parody in the business world: Survival of the Most Aggressive, Cutthroat, and Demanding. Perhaps you've been taught or told that transparency is overrated. That it is for the weak, for beginners, or for those who can't "hide" their tracks.

You know better.

CONCLUSION

"I am not afraid of an army of lions led by a sheep;
I am afraid of an army of sheep led by a lion."
—Alexander the Great

People have often asked me, "If there was just *one* principle that you could choose to implement, which one would it be?"

My answer is, all of them.

If you don't know where to start, take a tiny assessment quiz. Score yourself on a scale of 1 to 5 (1 = weak, 5 = strong) on focus, accountability, simplicity, and transparency, then put your greatest effort on the weakest link.

Of course, they are all interconnected. By immersing yourself in one, you are bound to improve in others. But the order of these principles matters. Focus comes first—what's the point of hitting the wrong dartboard? But simplicity and transparency lend themselves to focus, just as focus and transparency lend themselves to simplicity, and so forth.

A few years ago, I was asked to take over the IT operations of a major manufacturing company. Their performance was lacking, and the skyrocketing operational costs were not reflecting the poor quality of service.

When I took over the department, I reviewed the operational costs and performance. They'd tried some initiatives, including outsourcing, trying to save up to 20 million euros per annum. They didn't expect a higher level of quality. It appeared be an attempt to get the same mess for less—at still too high a price. The entire department was dangerously lacking in focus, simplicity, transparency, and accountability.

Management had been focusing on the overall financial numbers, wondering if they were meeting their 200-million-euro budget. New initiatives were repeatedly being jumpstarted in order to "improve things," but these went down like dominos; since there was never a real understanding of the problems, it was difficult to come up with simple solutions that people could understand and deliver. I estimated that we could increase the initial cost reduction target, saving up to 40 million euros, if we set the right focus and implemented a certain degree of transparency.

The teams were overworked, uninspired, and frustrated. It was little wonder that they were underperforming. Worst of all, nobody had been willing to accept accountability within the department's many poorly performing sectors.

It was time for a change. I began with a strategy conference with the fifty staff members of the senior leadership team. The most important thing we could do—and did—was define our two key goals:

1. To reduce operational costs by 40 million euros annually over the next four years.

2. To improve optimal performance.

The operational performance, unlike the cost target, was not as starkly measurable, of course. Nevertheless, the leadership team realized they had to end *everything* that didn't either lead to a reduction in cost or an improvement in operational performance. By the end of this one meeting, they knew what to communicate to their own teams, they knew what success looked like, and they'd rekindled their motivation. They thanked me for providing clarity.

Defining the focus enabled us to continue on to the other principles. Accountability was easy to assign but difficult to enforce due to the lack of transparency in individual team performance. Therefore, we assigned individual team responsibilities across the sectors (Supply Chain, Finance, Human Resources, Data Centers, etc.). The regional heads became accountable for cost and performance within their regions, while the functional heads became accountable for costs and operations within their function.

By creating a series of performance reports, we revealed each team's operating performance and implemented regular review meetings to compare measurements. Initially, we uncovered a nightmare of data errors. The mere act of transparency—tracking the information and holding the teams accountable—resulted in drastic clean-up and improvements. Once the information was available and accurate, the teams immediately improved the quality. Once the teams were able to see and manage costs at the 1- to 5-thousand-euro level, rather than the 5- to 10-million-euro level, it was far easier to spot excess spending.

To increase accountability and focus, we aligned employee bonuses with these key performance indicators.

Each team was rewarded based on its own performance, and their rewards were aligned with the overall department performance. It was a win-win for everyone involved.

It took three months to see tangible results. The marked improvement began to propel the teams forward faster and faster, motivating them with confidence. Within a year, the company had significantly transformed the operational performance (improving it over 50 percent), made some significant savings (surpassing the 40-million-euro mark), and continued to willingly increase its breadth of transparency. Given all this, we were able to identify and achieve even more areas of improvement.

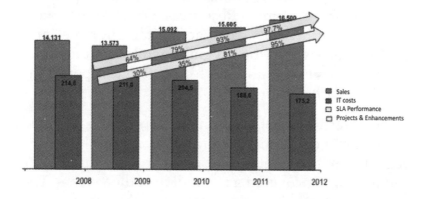

By implementing four simple principles—FAST—this multi-million-euro business, like many others, completely changed its fate.

I think it's your turn.

Lion-Hearted Leadership

Leadership is no laughing matter. It is not a task for the weak or the meek.

With great power comes great responsibility.

One of my favorite leadership quotes was spoken by one of the greatest military leaders in history, Alexander the Great, when he was asked what he feared. "I am not afraid of an army of lions led by a sheep," he replied. "I am afraid of an army of sheep led by a lion." He understood that leadership has the power to morph an army of sheep into a force to be reckoned with—a force powerful enough to defeat an army of lions. For under the right mentor and in the right conditions, even a team of sheep can become a team of lions.

Just by studying this book and reading to the end, you have proven something very valuable to me: you have the dedication to pursue something, as well as the passion to believe that it's possible. You care enough for your business's growth to seek a solution. You care enough about your own self-development to understand that *change* equals *growth,* and as humans we are always meant to *keep learning.*

If the four principles of the FAST strategy appealed to you, I believe that you will have no trouble implementing them and reaping the immediate and astounding benefits, as so many others before you. If you have the willingness to include more focus, accountability, simplicity, and transparency in your own life, I am confident that you will be able to use the methodologies outlined throughout this book in order to influence your teams and uplift your business.

FAST Quick Start

Here are 20 quick tips to get you started.

Focus

1. Keep the goals and targets to a minimum; between three to five works best in my experience.

2. Review goals and targets, making sure they are clear, simply explained, and well understood.

3. Review the solution, approach, or process in detail to ensure whether or not it will lead to the desired results if successfully executed. If not, change it.

4. Get the solution reviewed by a third party, either an external or an internal such as internal audit, and ask them to check that the focus is right.

5. Communicate clearly, simply, and often to the team to ensure that everyone understands the goals and that everyone is aligned.

Accountability

1. Identify clear roles and responsibilities, with clear expectations of what is required from that role.

2. Hold people accountable for outcomes and results, not for following processes.

3. Hold regular review meetings; these let people know that they will be held accountable.

4. Provide reward and recognition for jobs well done.

5. Be accountable yourself.

Simplicity

1. Don't stop at the first solution you find; complex solutions are easy to find, but simple ones are the best.

2. Challenge your teams, and especially experts, and ask if there is there a "pencil solution."

3. Make sure the solution is simply explained and easily understood.

4. Challenge everything; if it's not needed, rip it out.

5. Use Pareto. Look to complete 80 percent of the work in the first 20 percent of the time.

Transparency

1. Ensure you fully understand 100 percent of what is involved to be successful.

2. Create a plan that progress can be measured against.

3. Ensure each team has its own fact-based progress report.

4. Hold regular progress meetings with each team.

5. Communicate progress regularly to your teams.

FAST is a simple approach, but we must not confuse simple with easy. All goals, especially worthwhile goals, require hard work, and if you take a FAST approach, you will significantly increase your rate of success.

In this book, I have covered a lot of material, but in all honesty, I have barely scratched the surface.

If you want to learn more about FAST, then checkout my website, www.gordontredgold.com, where you will find more information about upcoming FAST courses, workshops, and events.

ABOUT THE AUTHOR

Gordon Tredgold, known as the Leader's Leader, *inspires leaders to develop engaged teams with clear plans so they can revolutionize their results.*

Gordon has always had the unique ability to assess difficult situations, determine what could be done differently, and then create simple, easy to understand, and easy to implement solutions that deliver sustainable results—FAST.

Originally from Leeds, England, Gordon's early passions were rugby and mathematics. Although he was usually one of the smallest players, Gordon loved to lead from the front, surprising his bigger opponents with his technique and tenacity. As others discovered his analytical skills, he helped people to identify a different and more effective way to do things. Combined with his passion for being part of a winning team, Gordon soon turned his skills into a professional purpose.

At the start of his career, Gordon was keen for rapid advancement and decided to take on the most difficult challenges available—the tough jobs that no one else wanted to do or that people thought would fail. He recognized these opportunities as a FAST way to rise through the ranks. Knowing that nothing succeeds as quickly as success, Gordon believed that triumphing in areas where other people thought it couldn't be done was the best use of his analytical skills and his fierce determination to succeed. This approach allowed him to challenge traditional thinking and come up with innovative solutions.

Both rapid advancement and results followed, and ever since *Gordon has worked with companies all over the world, leading them to revolutionary results that have created stronger, more efficient teams, raising up leaders for the new millennium and, ultimately, delivering a positive impact on bottom line revenue.*

Focusing on turnarounds, operational excellence, transformational change, and strategic implementation, Gordon is passionate about *identifying simple methodologies that can be quickly implemented and generate immediate benefits for people and companies.*

With a particular expertise in Driving Change, Service Delivery, and a variety of core competencies—including Target and Project Management, Strategic Analysis, Process Improvements and Best Practices, Technology and Business Linkage Planning, Capital Planning and Investment Control, and C+ Levels and Board of Management Liaison—Gordon is *the authority* on getting *FAST* results His nearly thirty years of expertise, work experience on three continents, and leading global teams and careers with billion-dollar companies such as Henkel, Deutsche Post DHL, and Cable and Wireless have won him worldwide accolades and the distinguished honor of being recognized as the Number One Leadership Expert to follow on Twitter.

Heralded in *Inc. Magazine* as one of the top 100 Leadership and Management Experts and Speakers, Gordon is also ranked #2 on the *Top 15 Must Read Leadership Blogs* and #4 on the *Top 50 Most Socially Shared Leadership Blogs*. He is also a visiting professor at Staffordshire University, a Fellow of the Institute of Leadership and Management, and a member of the National Speakers Association.

Gordon provides both consulting and coaching services, and works with groups and individuals. He is the author of two books on leadership, and is currently working on his third.

For more information or to contact Gordon Tregold visit him at:

Twitter: @gordontredgold
Facebook: www.facebook.com/leadershipprinciples

Email: gordon@leadership-principles.com

Groups can connect with Gordon and other like minded FAST leaders on:

Facebook: www.facebook.com/groups/FASTLeader/

Linkedin: www.linkedin.com/grp/home?gid=6968072 or search for "FAST Leaders" i n the groups page